SIX-WAY MIRROR

ROBERT SAXTON was born in Nottingham in 1952.
He lives in north London, where he works as a freelance
editor and writer. He is the author of five previous books of
poetry: from Enitharmon, *The Promise Clinic* (1994); from
Carcanet/OxfordPoets, *Manganese* (2003), *Local Honey* (2007)
and *Hesiod's Calendar* (2010); and from Shearsman, *The China
Shop Pictures* (2012). He is also represented in Faber's *Poetry
Introduction 7* and Carcanet's *Oxford Poets 2001* anthology.
In 2001 he won the Keats-Shelley Memorial Association's
poetry prize for 'The Nightingale Broadcasts'.

See **www.robertsaxton.co.uk** for more information.

SIX-WAY MIRROR

Robert Saxton

For Jenny
love from
Bob

Robert Saxton
26 June 2018

ANGLE SHADES
PRESS

Published in 2016 by
Angle Shades Press

in association with Albury Books
Albury Court, Albury, Thame,
Oxfordshire, OX9 2LP
www.alburybooks.com

A CIP catalogue record for this title is available from the British Library

Printed and bound by CPI Group (UK) Ltd, Croydon, CR0 4YY
ISBN 978-1-910571-58-3 (paperback)

ACKNOWLEDGEMENTS
I am grateful to the Society of Authors for a generous grant that enabled me to finish
and revise this book.

Thanks also to:
Manisha Patel for her excellent typographic and cover design, as well as her sensitivity
and understanding;
Angela Young of Albury Books (Imago) for publishing and production help and wisdom;
Hannah Howell of Albury for her friendly skill and efficiency on the IT/sales side.

for David and Rachel

'That which has no substance can penetrate that
which has no opening.'

Tao Te Ching, chapter 43

'You shall listen to all sides and filter them from
yourself.'

'All truths wait in all things,
They neither hasten their own delivery, nor resist it...'

Walt Whitman, 'Song of Myself',
sections 1 and 30, *Leaves of Grass*

CONTENTS

INTRODUCTION

Six-way Mirror is conceived as a poem rather than as a collection of poems. However, this does not imply that the reader is expected to progress through the work in page order in the usual way. The structure of the poem is panoptic: there is no line of narrative or logic requiring a linear approach. No doubt, as with a collection, many readers will be inclined to be selective, delving at random within the text, or focusing on specific topics that attract their interest. Some may prefer to read conventionally, from the beginning. However, for the guidance of any who would like to try reading systematically in the spirit of the fictive principle that underlies the poem, a set of 64 hexagrams is attributed to 64 headings in a manner that will be familiar to anyone acquainted with the I Ching.

Following the customary usage of that ancient Chinese text, the reader is invited to toss three coins six times, using the resulting permutations of heads and tails to cast a hexagram – a graphic figure of six horizontal lines in a vertical stack. In certain circumstances, as described below, the hexagram thus derived will yield a secondary hexagram alongside it. Each hexagram, linked to a specific theme, directs the reader towards a particular section of the poem with which he or she then engages.

The content and intention of *Six-way Mirror* have little relation to the I Ching. This was not planned as a work of divination or spiritual wisdom; and no attempt is made to generate a Chinese atmosphere. Accordingly, the method of approaching the book suggested below does not mimic I Ching procedure precisely: indeed it departs radically from the classic method after the initial hexagram has been cast. For anyone who wishes to read more of the poem than one or two of the 64 sections, my method takes a turn towards the numerological, following a simple practice that is quicker and less tiresome than repeated coin throwing. From this point onwards your reading is shaped not by chance but by a pathway encoded into each of the hexagrams like DNA. You unfold this pathway by working with a chart, which serves also as a quick-reference index for the hexagrams, directing you to the numbered sections (cantos) of the poem.

To readers who wonder why they should go to the trouble of casting a hexagram and then following a chart, rather than dipping into the poem serendipitously or reading it all the way through, I offer the following response, articulated from the heart of the project.

When an arrangement of passages for reading is made by a procedure that incorporates the operation of chance, the result will be a specific text for that particular reader at that particular time. In this case, if the method is applied to all 64 sections, a distinctively ordered version of the whole poem will be created. Or if the method is applied to fewer sections, a poem within the poem is revealed: a micro poem within the macro. The macro poem is conceived as a holistic organism, not as a linear sequence, and this gives authenticity to a 'cutting': it is hoped that any segment, or series of segments, will partake of the vitality of the whole.

Six-way Mirror has been devised as a territory, not a journey. Thought has been given to the order of themes: in fact, they form in themselves a kind of mirror, whose reflective surface falls at the half-way point (32/33). However, the thematic organisation, with its 64 numbered sections, is intended to function like a grid on a map: it helps you to navigate; it has no substantive significance.

In the absence of a single prescribed route, a reader given licence to roam, without an itinerary, would surely be entitled to feel somewhat abandoned. Inevitably, chance played a large part in the writing; on the other hand, the poem's subject, in part, is the logic of cause and effect,

9

in a variety of circumstances. A reading method that in a precise way brings together chance and causation, even if the reader exercises his or her right not to follow it, is integral to the enterprise as a whole. This method is not a courteous afterthought gifted by the poet to the reader but a quasi-neurological system that has made poetic thought possible in the first place.

Browsing freely within the book would also, it is true, bring causative factors into play, but they would be elusively personal to the reader, or elusively circumstantial, or a mysterious mixture of the two. There is infinite scope for the subjective in the reader's *response* to *Six-way Mirror*. Hence, the rest of this introduction is taken up with proposing a reading method that excludes the subjective and narrows down the circumstantial to comprehensible limits.

Casting a hexagram

You begin by tossing three coins, all together, six times. After each of the six triple tosses you contribute a line to the hexagram, building it up from the bottom. The line will be either broken (yin) or unbroken (yang) according to the permutation of heads and tails shown by the throw:

2 heads, 1 tail	unbroken	———
3 heads	unbroken (changing line)	———
2 tails, 1 head	broken	— —
3 tails	broken (changing line)	— —

If your hexagram includes any changing lines, you draw a second hexagram alongside it. This supplementary hexagram is identical to the first, except that the changing lines are transformed into their opposites – broken where the first hexagram has unbroken, and vice versa.

Here is an example of how a particular set of throws results in a
primary hexagram with a supplementary hexagram alongside (since the
second and fifth throws have prompted changing lines):

6th throw: 2 h + 1 t	———	———
5th throw: 3 h	——— (changing)	— —
4th throw: 2 t + 1 h	— —	— —
3rd throw: 2 t + 1 h	— —	— —
2nd throw: 3 h	——— (changing)	— —
1st throw: 2 h + 1 t	———	———

Selecting and reading a canto

The poem is organised into 64 numbered cantos, each of which
comprises a rubric (almost all of these are imaginary quotations),
a preamble and seven numbered stanzas (paragraphs).

Having cast your first hexagram for a reading session, consult the
hexagram index chart overleaf (or on the last page of the book) to find
the numbered canto to which it refers. The upper trigrams (three-line
figures) of the hexagrams are arranged along the horizontal axis and
the lower trigrams along the vertical axis. Where the relevant axes
meet, locate the canto number (in lieu of a page number), turn to the
canto indicated and begin your reading. Read the whole canto – rubric,
preamble and all seven stanzas. Then, if your hexagram included one or
more changing lines, read the stanzas that correspond to those particular
lines a second time, with additional concentration: these are, as it were,
the foreground features of the canto, expressing a primary meaning.
(Remember that '1st' means the first line you drew, which is the one at

	☰	☳	☵	☶	☷	☴	☲	☱
☰	1	34	5	26	11	9	14	43
☳	25	51	3	27	24	42	21	17
☵	6	40	29	4	7	59	64	47
☶	33	62	39	52	15	53	56	31
☷	12	16	8	23	2	20	35	45
☴	44	32	48	18	46	57	50	28
☲	13	55	63	22	36	37	30	49
☱	10	54	60	41	19	61	38	58

the bottom of the hexagram; and that '6th' is the top line.) It is unlikely that all six lines in your hexagram will be changing lines, but if they are, the foreground meaning is to be found in the last stanza, entitled 'All six'.

Next, if you have cast a second hexagram based on the changing lines in the first, look up the corresponding canto number in the same way. Again, give extra emphasis in your reading to the lines that have changed.

Continuing the reading

To determine your route for further reading, consult the hexagram index chart again and re-locate within its grid the number of the canto to which your first hexagram directed you. From that square count off seven further squares, proceeding horizontally from left to right. If you reach the right-hand edge of the grid, make a 180-degree turn, downwards, and continue your count along the adjacent row beneath, in the opposite direction. The seventh square you land on, after jumping the six-square interval, directs you to the next canto for reading. Continue in this way, plotting your route through the grid and reading, in their entirety, each of the cantos whose squares you land on. Turn 180 degrees downwards at the left-hand edge of the grid whenever you encounter it and double back as before. Your pathway will be continuous until you reach the end of the grid (bottom corner square): at that point jump up vertically to the top and continue your counting, whether to the left or to the right, along the top row.

If you happen to land again on the supplementary hexagram, whose corresponding canto you will have read already, use it merely as a stepping stone from which to execute a further seven-square leap; do not re-read the text for that hexagram unless you particularly wish to.

Concluding the reading

The advantage of leaping repeatedly over six squares to land on the seventh is that you will be able to do this uninterruptedly for seven circuits of the grid, covering all its squares without ever landing on the same square twice. If your aim is to read a complete version of the macro poem (all 64 cantos), this is a neat procedure to follow.

If you prefer to commit less time to your reading and confine yourself to one of the micro poems, you might find this more satisfying if you decide on the number of cantos in the micro poem beforehand. I would suggest you take six as a suitable number – or twelve, or eighteen. Or you might decide to complete a single circuit of the grid, since this will give you a satisfying ten cantos (not counting any supplementary canto if your initial hexagram yielded changing lines). All these extents are to be taken as authorised micro poems.

However, there is no reason why you should not go off-piste and devise your own unauthorised micro poem of a different extent, using any variation of the coin-throwing and numerological methods, or any other method you might choose to invent for yourself.

(Of course, with the grid method, instead of progressing rightwards and downwards you could, if you wish, work leftwards and upwards, or upwards and leftwards, or in any other direction available to you. These options might be of interest if you wish to explore alternative versions of a micro or macro poem, all starting from the same hexagram.)

The changing lines

In the suggested procedure described above, the changing lines have a part to play only at the start of the reading. However, another (hereby authorised) approach to *Six-way Mirror* would be to use coin throwing to generate a handful of hexagrams – let's say three, which after all may possibly yield twice that number if changing lines appear. Given the narrower focus provided by three to six cantos, or even four to eight, you are more likely to derive an additional layer of interest from the foregrounding of the changing lines, as previously described. It is in short, concentrated readings, and particularly divinatory readings, that the changing lines come into their own. For those open-minded about chance, intuition and destiny, and the possible connections between them, it might be fruitful to experiment with the poem as an instrument – a mirror – for oracular introspection in the manner of the I Ching. I lay no claim to clairvoyant talents. But if a tree does not know how to dance, the wind will sometimes teach it.

SIX-WAY MIRROR

the 64 cantos

1

THE MIRROR

'Look both ways before you cross yourself. Gaze first at the hills in the picture and then at the picture made by the hills.'

Eureka! The crackpot scientist brandishes his formula: seven shards of light at right angles to flowing water. Only by running around the back of his mind could he take his panoptic self-portrait. Each morning he checks deep into the corners for stowaways. In the green tank hangs a fish shimmering beyond the reach of artifice, waiting to regain its soul shape.

1st – The Mirror of Illusion
Despite global axes we relate to an object locally. Up and down are the same in both systems. Rotation is a fiction of our body's left-right symmetry. Raise your north hand: your reflection does the same. Right and left; cardinal points. The mirror's strangeness is down to language.

2nd – The Mirror of Beauty
The frame's wrinkles accumulate a detritus of process, drifting like sand. The eye, trained in compassion, smiles at beauty tiptoeing inwards, the seasons truthfully turning. What's seen can never be unseen; what's stale can never be fresh again. Entropy: a new cream for rejuvenating the mind.

3rd – The Accidental Mirror

It's perilous in the urban battlefield: you catch yourself out in a fusillade of light, a stranger suddenly revealed as your surrogate, caught unawares. Your mind is clouds around disfiguring lightning. There's a rip in the camouflage net of the high street – instantly mended and forgotten.

4th – The Forsaken Mirror

It's obvious, you can't stay inside yourself all day, polishing your axioms. Time-limit your reflection. Self-regard is a gateway, like having to undress behind a bush before swimming. Don the silver head-wings. Spread them in the threat position if you must. Then relax into the self-created dream.

5th – The Mermaid's Mirror

The comb and mirror are vital: what else could she do with her hands? Metamorphosis travels upwards from the tail fin to the intertidal zone of the midriff. A schoolgirl in mermaid costume, perched on a rock for the prince's helicopter fly-past, evaluates the fading love bite on her neck.

6th – The Rearview Mirror

The mirror is always our guardian, our third eye, as when a bear obscures the sun behind us while we drink from the pond, or when a new lover looms, his chest a rampant creeper, hands outstretched to settle on your shoulders. How else control the rebellious third child at the family table?

All six – The Cosmic Mirror

There's a personal flow and there's a cosmic order. The salmon may be landed in its ladder or loved in the arc of its exuberance. Think of the self, analogous. The orchestra's finest moment is the point of break-up. The toyless pram, marooned in the street, overflows with musical tears.

2

THE FRIEND

'Alphabetical seating arrangements at the police academy encourage alphabetical groups of friends, with congestion in address books.'

A mishap in the tanning booth leaves him with an over-tanned front. It will be slow to fade, though his paler back can be darkened if he'll risk the machine again. This duo – left-brain and right-brain bromance – work all night on their script, vibrant with tanning lore, baseball history, coffee shop capers. They mount the stage together at the comedy awards.

1st – The Temporary Friends
Weighing his possibilities, he looks each way – at the student bar, at the stately pile. Down for the weekend, they have emptied decanters in the library, searched for a *faux* book about trout fishing, with money inside. Gravely he accepts from Pa the Remington he used to write his memoirs.

2nd – The Friend and Colleague
A checked shirt discomforts striped and plain alike – striped being honorary vanilla. Convention retention bows to the powers that be. Yet brilliance sparks off any unexpectedness, like a drill bit glancing off a diamond. All this is careless talk, without which careful talk will plod.

3rd – The Friends Who Have Shared the Darkness

They have run around in battle without their chainmail, screaming; yet
have known poetry flying the beautiful Hooey. And still they carry the
risks, the psychic scars. Entering a public toilet, he too has to kick open
the doors of all the cubicles before being able to turn his back at the urinal.

4th – The Friends of Track and Field

The coin notorious for breaking asunder, with a cupro-nickel centre and a
nickel-brass surround, inspires their brainwave. One came first, the other
second, in the greatest race of their lives – but the judges got it wrong.
Melting down their gold and silver medals, they mint two equal hybrids.

5th – The Fair-weather Friends

The hotel terrace is a court, the jury outside in the sun. The toxicology
of opprobrium is still not fully understood. How will she find a husband,
calibrating the stars for three years and still ending up without a degree?
How will she take her place in the yoke of the wagon of endurance?

6th – The Friends of the Penultimate Days

Smiles seed in the ruins of infrastructure. Winter's broken thermometers
litter the old holloways – the trade routes, the highways to an old
sweetheart. Sarcasm becomes competitive, before collapsing back on
itself in empathy, defying the dog days' dental records, the world's snarl.

All six – The Friend from the Pool of Youth

A face half familiar on the college lawn, a light intelligence. Then memory
dawns: the architectural conservationist, famous for illicit turf dwellings
vandalised by reactionaries. Though never close, they have swum in a pool
of golden light, and droplets fall from them still at their reunion.

3

THE MOTH

'There is nothing to be gained, not even justice, by putting on trial the moth that has eaten the tapestry. It warrants the same amnesty as a rust moth.'

Our own lives may seem crepuscular in the wisdom of a warm summer night. Yet the dust on Castaneda's moth, loose on its powdery wing, is no dull shower of bookish sediment but quick bright knowledge shaken from a *vita breva* – the Latin taking flight from common parlance, beating itself ragged against a scholar's lamp, too desperate to give up the ghost.

1st – The Moth of Reason
As Darwinists are drawn to a Bunsen flame, creationists are born again in Jerusalem. Forget black morphs on sooty chimneys: white ones on bark stripped of lichen are blatant to birds. The research was flawed. Many were placed on trunks in daylight; some were dead, and glued there.

2nd – The Moth Migration
Capitol Hill, with its floodlit rotunda and flagpole, is a lightning rod for seasonal panic. Once a year Parliament is infested: a lift jams, fire alarms are triggered. In cafés many drown in saucers of tea. At the opera house pale agitated high notes enliven the soprano in her spotlight.

3rd – The Names of the Moth
The anthology *par excellence*, beyond criticism, is a selection of our macro moth names, with plates or the memory of plates. Swallow prominent, Angle shades, The drinker, Feathered thorn, Oak lutestring, Powdered quaker, Dingy shears – Miltonic in the hedgerows of Paradise.

4th – The Clothes Moth
Nordic sweater patterns – stylised derricks, spouting whales – replace tartans this far north of the clan line. Moths are like postcards from a lowland aunt, unread till she's passed away. A *fashionista* better half calculates that if there's wool around, maybe they won't eat silk.

5th – The Death's-head Hawkmoth
Many of the sightings in the city that year were prompted by shrieks, which some believed to be the death cries the braveheart king had stoppered in his throat at the Tower. Often they sneaked past the guards in hives, mimicking the scent of bees while gluttonising nectar and honey.

6th – The Moth in Heat
A squadron trapped in the revolving doors of the west campus, catching an irresistible puff of molecules, the pheromone plume, hurriedly they fling themselves a country mile to a female in the hanging position, wings ajar to expose her abdomen's hind end, urgent glistening gland extruded.

All six – The Moth Campaign
From a mini-cosmos of harm falls a rain of toxic caterpillar hairs, onto dog walkers, nature lovers. A helicopter scutters low over the oak wood but not until after the school run. In the event, collateral damage is limited to nature: White admiral, Silver-washed fritillary, Scarlet tiger moth.

4

THE PRINCESS

'That was no lipstick: it was a chip she'd dipped in ketchup. A tiara would have been the height of vulgarity.'

Imagine if her buckle spelled 'Peace' or bore the Toyota glyph unwittingly; or she named her daughter Toya. Not on your royal jelly! The palace is omniscient these days. Even the secret tattoo is chronicled and parsed, and indeed is the subject of a no less secret report. Anxiety, however, is devolved: that's the business of the royal household.

1st – The Future Princess
She fences deftly with her moral tutor, a feminist luminary, expert in literary economics. Meeting His Holiness at a charity disco, she makes an indelible impression. A provocative and compelling Titania, she dislikes her Bottom, a mechanical roué on the make, seducing himself on stage.

2nd – The Princess in Love
Much in the public eye, the young lovers smoulder in a restaurant after weeks apart. He's in uniform, a colonel still. She adores that asymmetric smile with its twist of inborn shyness. Security harrumphs. There's something on the menu that sounds rude, so of course she has to order it.

3rd – The Frog Princess

The Fabergé barouche or the Waterford landau? While she's dithering,
the prince makes a bonfire of her frog skin, unaware that her amphibious
probation is only days from full term. A clot of pigeons masks the sun.
Rioters swarm through the Tuileries. The whole world changes hands.

4th – The Princess of Darkness

Fireworks explode in the night: a startled exit from a taxi. The other side
is a private cloud of unknowing, whose raindrops are the only pearls left.
A meteoric alpha commoner has emptied her portfolio, stripping their
waltz of all but the quavers of romance, and making it more passionate.

5th – The Travelling Princess

You swim in her bridal grief-song, a lake of yearning in the forest. There's
jumping – over a broomstick, a boiling kettle, a bowl of wine and urine.
Two weeks later her train is the longest ever, flowing down the aisle, a
river, out through doors left open all through the ceremony.

6th – The Princess of Charity

A lifeguard for the national gene pool, she enjoys robots designed by
children fighting with each other, bloodlessly. Other kids she weans off
parkour. Raiments of Wicca fluttering still, she turns to animals, sluicing
the manger of the butcher-*perfumiers* – a clean sweep of fragrance.

All six – The Intimate Princess

The young pretender's underlook is the apparatus of sincerity, the
crown jewels of suffering. The princess steps nimbly onto the high wire,
embarrassing the Commonwealth's living rooms. Fame forfeits the right
to a net. Magna Carta's small print is scattered to the four winds.

5

THE TEAPOT

'A second brew needs a helping hand, so shift your arse and serve me, Jeeves!
Lift that lid and stir those leaves.'

Drinking tea directly from the spout, as the Chinese did in antiquity, releases the flavour of addiction. Teapots were smaller then, scaled for the individual. His brew crock stolen, perhaps by a rival, the philosopher is drained of poetry. The taste now is alien – bony and bitter. Petition the Forbidden City: nothing is impossible for a raging thirst like this.

1st – The Mysterious Teapot
What would happen without that tiny hole in the lid? Bad air built up like tea behind a dam would send a cataract of pulses spluttering through the spout, as if trying to expel words through a gag of social anxiety. Trivia question: is it true some reckless teapots dispense with a proper spiracle?

2nd – The Predictable Teapot
No precautions are deemed necessary. Repeating its philistine spillage, a trickle down the spout like a moneylender's chin, this incorrigible vessel stains cambric with the sabotage you always expected – as if walking in a fresh fall of snow and never once looking back at your footprints.

3rd – The Villager's Teapot

A parishioner's annual chore. 'More tea, vicar?' Her question has perfect
pitch, an irony caught only by intimates. A good shrine needs no blush.
Silent as an angel's bloodstream, the room collects trumps and tinkles.
In this quarter-way house to heaven animal vestments somewhat chafe.

4th – The Teapot on a Trestle Table

This rich brown warhorse off the assembly line, ignorable household
genie, exerts an insouciant gravity that kept a family from flying apart. It's
a pragmatic system: toxins trapped as flecks beneath the glaze and a spout
pouring double-strength tonic. 'Buy me and gruffly heal your hurts.'

5th – The Rococo Teapot

Monkey violinists akimbo among flying pheasants and pendant peaches
are a triumph of the Trianon's will. Fingers perform six impossible swirls
at breakfast and tea. The minister of culture, peering up from beneath a
glass table, wittily frenchifies its provenance: the mosses of Saxony.

6th – The Rustic Teapot

The windows are tax-avoiding solids, one with a painted hobbit. The
knob's a crooked chimney in the thatch; the handle, an Oedipal tree trunk.
How to naturalise the spout? A banished wood sprite, innovative drainage,
or an unmentionable elephant's trunk stretching out to drink the rain?

All six – The Teapot in the Souk

After the fuss of welcome, carpets are rumbled out with a flourish,
crisscrossing, tightening the commitment to consider. Then mint tea is
brought, in a lamp-like pot with octagonal windows. Mint is the aroma
of transaction. Only a Berber could walk out at this point with dignity.

6

THE OAK TREE

'Lady Gregory's earthly nightmare: the crash of the acorn, and the roots jostling each other rudely through the cleft.'

An Arthurian oak ship, sailing the seven centuries, is under attack from aliens. The bark emits a gall that traps every familiar monster in a spherical prison – a setback so habitual it alters the course of evolution. Sealing off a whole wing is no more heroic. Why carry an oak deck no longer needed? Why not starve it of sap to conserve precious resources?

1st – **The Royal Oak**
Stormtroopers, riding among the junipers, discover the rebels' armoury sharing a hollow veteran of the forest with a woodpecker – but not the once-and-future king on a trampoline of ropes in his loosening upper chamber, in woodsman's attire, kept awake by a retainer's elbow.

2nd – **The Humanitarian Oak**
A knuckle of oak from one of the patrol ships, fashioned into a pen holder, was gifted from PM Brown to President Obama. Naval sea dogs harry piratical wolves. Shackles are never found on board: the evidence tends to be timber en route to Africa – a slave deck not yet assembled.

3rd – The Oak of Sustenance

It's morning in paradise! Holm acorns like starfruit on branches springing
the timeless space around Grand Tour antiquities crated in Greece and
shipped to Holkham are grown in the park by gardeners' thrift. Their
succulent yield is freighted to London, fodder for the zoo's giraffes.

4th – The Forgotten Oak Wood

A bogeymen stalks an abandoned munitions factory – by the time the
oaks had grown to maturity, stunted and sick, ironclads bore down on
rebel colonies. A child of these woods might soon lose his innocence,
swiping with a cricket bat at a lover's heart pierced by an ogre's arrow.

5th – The Collegiate Oak

It's far from sporting to shut this massive door, no doubt the valve to a
conclave or an orgy. The carvings are cuttings from Rousseau's garden,
with serpents and squirrels frolicking together in the foliage. From the
biome of moral experiment so many promising students are expelled.

6th – The Oak Sapling as a Weed

Acorns drop and are hoarded; some are flung. We separate ourselves
from spent enthusiasms, including the sonnet's perfection (warty octave,
smooth, shiny sestet). We might find one in a pocket with our keys, which
explains their favoured habitat – front gardens likelier than back.

All six – The Cacophonous Oak

This is the harvest festival of the species, the week when caterpillars
munch in their leafy larder. On a still day a woman hears jaws above her,
a mumbled satisfaction, getting louder as her hearing sifts frequencies.
At such attunement men can only gawp – incredulous, unengaged.

7

THE WINDOW

'Window table competition is a major cause of restaurant violence. Secure in our tenure, we gaze into each other's eyes.'

Check for visual tunnels birds may imagine they can fly through. Keep your windows slightly dirty to emasculate reflections. After a burglary, angle a new window downwards – check first that your warranty won't be compromised. The crowning touch is to stick on a replica orb-weaver spider's white zigzag *stabilimentum*, bird-hating centre of her web.

1st – The Window into History
She hugs him as if one or the other were a Ming vase – ironic in this upper-floor chamber where the two imperial governors and their secretary were pushed out of a window. They landed in a dung heap with just a few bruises. No one was harmed until the long war that followed.

2nd – The Witch Window
It's unlikely that delinquent spirits are troubled by angles – beware of fashioning otherness in your own suburban image. The point, however, is sacrifice. Tight between rooflines, the sloping misfit double sash testifies to godliness defying seemliness – a strongman between temple columns.

3rd – The Window Marking Time

The aspect is southerly. A guard consoles: 'This is no temperate land
where you could scratch the walls to chart the solstices. But there'll be
sudden storms, filling the cell with light and noise, freshening murderous
heat.' On the rack of a rainbow she sickens in the endless moment.

4th – The Window Seat

Dust from the quarry is treasured in the timeless vehicle of a raindrop,
intuiting its descent. Any pictures form in the head – the glowing logs
are behind her, only radiating, never reflecting. Rain and fire. Her body is
twisted awry from obvious solutions, away from the maddening hearth.

5th – The Window of Desire

The mannequins have that knowing look – defiant bald heads, slender
necks. This is far from the solidarity of sameness: even singletons triumph
over our muddles. Clothed ones are somehow naked underneath. They
are the perfect future, powerless to choose yet never compromised.

6th – The Window Tax

Water, light, air must be metered by a prudent state – though the principal
reason no doubt was ease of assessment. Loopholers, the Robin Hoods
of daylight, swing into action, trading favours with bricklayers. It takes
introverts only weeks to acclimatise to a life change; extraverts, years.

All six – The Window on the Northern Lights

When the vodka comes round, the talk is of time exposures. They mark
their places with tripods, on each one a card with a name and cell phone
number. Straight after lunch the village lights are dowsed. Protons arrive,
like aliens, on a solar wind, streaming through the Pole's magnetic sieve.

8

THE PRIEST

'A cold store within the furnace of the flesh; in the Arctic wastes of loss, a hearth, with a kitchen chair beside it.'

The priesthood is a reserve force, in training for the great resuscitation. Experts in living, they breathe in controversies, breathe out judgements, poring over the law of the world – its terse promulgations, its cryptic licences. Bodily punishments being no longer admissible, they invite wrongdoers into a labyrinth of mirrors. Their houses bulge with tractates.

1st – The Priestess
Planetary chaos, solar storms, ecliptic dust rage over the Nile. The head feathers of Amun are the consequent aurora. Sistrum-shaking, effigy-burning, mortally celibate Aset, revered wife and divine adoratrice, calls the greatest one to his meal. The sun god's hand is self-creatively female.

2nd – The Priest Who Knows Too Much
Voices float in the shadows, on the silence. How like the sensitivity of radio – a crime confessed for your ears only. Disbelieving, he interrogates a wedding ring, then a credit card, which he reads like braille: exhibits for blind heavenly assessment, in the court of inexhaustible permutations.

3rd – The Priest on the Eve of Battle

Communicants will drink black blood tomorrow. Known soldiers
are translated to the book of heroes. Truth makes the cross a roofless
sanctuary. Fingers trace escape routes in the air. The sky, raining damage,
is a counterfeit heaven. His flesh is the road, his blood the lubricating oil.

4th – The Anonymous Priest

'Forgive me, Father, for I have forgotten your name. Can you remember
mine?' Anonymity, some say, is the open sesame of the heart. A barrier
may be used as a bridge, a thoroughfare for a storm of assailants. The siege
begins with hypnosis, which only seems to strengthen the defences.

5th – The Priest in Jeopardy

He holds retreats in garages – the bag of tools under his arm is a folded
soutane. The vice tightens: many priests are forced to marry; or killed,
and buried without clergy. Laid out on his bed are photos of his enemies
torn from newspapers: he blesses them from the depths of his heart.

6th – The Priest of Track and Field

When two members of the club were electrocuted while restoring a
windmill, his help was intuitive, authentic and sustaining. More troubling
still is the way the game gets a grip on people, hollowing them out, like
religious zealotry. Cricket chaplains on call rush in from the outfield.

All six – The Priest Beatified

A drone reversed in the air and landed near a rebel village with a windfall
of supplies: engine, antennas, fuel cells. The nose-cone camera had
transmitted a crucifix: a hovering monk with his arms outstretched,
forbidding trespass. Now we fidget in limbo, awaiting the second miracle.

9

THE MARKET

'The skew is now the central cognitive aspect of option trading. The first thing you want to know when you walk into a pit is, What's the skew?'

His backpack slung on his chest, holding his nose, he tiptoes around large puddles – till the next tsunami sluices the floor. Live turtles, pickled ginseng, a cage of frogs, unlucky chicken's feet. Next day he brings his girlfriend. It's one of the new-fangled cleansing days, the elderly in disarray, troops in masks and white combat gear scanning for replicants.

1st – The Slave Market
His sketches capture sometimes submission, sometimes defiance: empathy or anger in the eyes. Slipping away, he dodges the crowd gathering its forces like an antibody. 'An Abolitionist, for sure. I'd pay a Negro twenty-five cents to send him on his way with his busted ass in his hands.'

2nd – The Market of Corrections
The comma tourists are out in force with their clipboards. This could almost be a wet test for the national curriculum, a spot of field study, risk-assessed, videoed for learning from mistakes. Later, stallholders pick apostrophes out of their banana's, like so many stowaway tarantulas.

3rd – **The Rain Market**
The ocean-going rig tacks across the square, sails bulging with rainwater,
sloshed out in bucketfuls. How did breadfruit get here, if not across a
storm-tossed sea? Some of these young blades refused the shilling. The
salty old lags, with doubloons in their blood, are not past wiving yet.

4th – **The Risk Market**
Glass ceiling jokes abound – there's a real one, a spidery dome like a
conservatory of the lost empire, a balloon sent up to scout for survivors.
Headwinds are modelled; *sentiment* is modelled. When algorithms fail,
you repress emotion, as you might if your spleen had let you down.

5th – **The Market at the Back of Beyond**
The empty quarter is mountains and plains, impossibly hot or cold.
Drones the size and weight of angels' wings are tested on a breeze-block
village in a quarry. Suits and uniforms mingle, cigars are compared, fire
water is drunk. Eagles soar. Handshakes are filmed in secret, from a satellite.

6th – **The Goblin Market**
Stolen ducal placentas, a termagant's vajazzle: antidotes to clarifying
crystals, diving beneath their radar. From one of these scales you can
grow a mermaid the size of a seahorse. 'Eat me, drink me, love me,'
shrieks a fruit from a desert oasis. Save the pips: seven will buy you a goblin.

All six – **The Spice Market**
This is bear root: first food of the bear awakened from hibernation.
This is copal, from lightning-struck trees: blood of forest beings. This is
cedar leaf: trauma is diffused with positive vibrations. This is sweet grass,
or mother's hair: it offers a prayer for a better world beyond thought.

10

THE GHOST

'A ghost who imitates the owl's hoot has misunderstood the moonlight.
The canny ghost gets hold of a sheet.'

On our side, seekers of asylum may find themselves in a cell of longing;
on theirs, there's an occasional mix-up over papers, or emotions may
serve as a one-way shuttle, earthwards. Some punishment may also be
involved, though the rules have never been codified. Transgressions are
recognised only by their intensity, the archer only by his sweetheart.

1st – The Ghost of Conscience
The imploring yelp in the pipework, the shoulder tap while you climb the
stairs, the peacock screen that has dragged itself out of the sun. What if
conscience is the culprit – that porcupine of arrows? Relax your mindful
attention. Turn the attic upside down, searching for a clean slate.

2nd – The Ghost of Public Resort
True evidence of a haunting encourages tomfoolery – tricks played on,
say, a new recruit in the bar, a student from Minsk. A wall with hunting
trinkets is easy enough for a ghost to walk through: arrow light shows it
well. Among so many counterfeits its limbo is ever more desolate.

3rd – The Telekinetic Ghost

Confusion among the living, muddled further by limited powers on the other side. An arrow cannot be pulled from its course, only fall short of its target; a vase cannot be emptied, only nudged off its shelf. The art is in its infancy. The soul in pain appears merely brattish, a spoilt child.

4th – The Invited Ghost

Expectation can manifest as knocks and shudders, and perhaps there's contact of sorts – a crackling comb-fest of invisible filaments, a timeshare of intention. An electric arrow spins on its axis of yearning. Galvanised picnickers feast off their winding sheet. Nutritional value: negligible.

5th – The Ghost with the Upper Hand

A spirit, clothed, may even smile in a bathroom at a naked person's discomfort. Then will follow the sudden vanishing, like a whoosh of arrows through the steam, leaving our witness with that aching incompleteness before telling such an urgent story for the first time.

6th – The Ghost of Persistent Life

The lattice stands tragically public: the vine has withered back into its root. At the molecular level there is no loss of energy – much of it parasitical. An arrow will cleave to its birth tree. No one can annihilate a memory – some fragment blooms in fury. The realm of severance teems.

All six – The Ghost Exorcised

This is serious: expunging a demonic life form requires anguished effort, far down in the fountainhead. Removing his purple stole, he puts on the white. Hands wet with his own spittle, he touches mouth and nose and tears the devil's arrow from the wound. Latin works intensely *in extremis*.

11

THE HONEY BEE

'When a bee comes to your house, let her have beer: you may wish to repay the compliment one day.' (Congolese proverb)

Outer workers shiver their wings to heat the ball; inner and outer swap in shifts. The queen winters in the middle. Between combs is a patented bee space, just letting two bees pass each other. The prize is a jar of balsam honey, born of seeds washed out of French and Spanish fleeces and swept downstream to found a colony of flowers on the bonny banks of the Tyne.

1st – The Hieroglyphic Bee

From his box of instruments he extracts a beeswax crocodile and slips it into the water where his wife's lover is bathing. Coming to life and growing big, it drags him down to the Nile's depths. The bee and the sedge: this dual key is the life force, nestled within the title of the king.

2nd – The Procreative Bee

The swarm was men, searching for ten nests in a wood of five hundred trees. One in a thousand died, falling. So now you'll find sections of trunk on the ground, as hives, and these have received our myths, of men and bears. The hole below the belt is a two-way portal of the vital spirit.

3rd – The Enlightened Bee

A well-hung monarchy needs its bee books – spate of good works, noble inventions. Queen Henrietta Maria, dedicatee of dozens, took one with her when she fled the falling shadow of the axe, re-inscribing it to her protectors. Its final sanctuary was Napoleon's cabinet of curiosities.

4th – The Aggressive Bee

That waft of banana attracts more bees to the sting, till the hapless mink is mobbed. Sacs pump away like severed heads revising their last menu. Trouble's in the air. A queen stings rival queens. A wasp is balled – overheated in the bees' clump and fumed with their carbon dioxide.

5th – The Frontier Bee

Honey bees glimpsed at the edges of confusion. Westwards they drive the tribes and the buffalo – hostile air force of the paleskin robbers, their hum the death rattle of sacred silence. The shaman warns, 'We will learn the shrunken sweetness, the subjection of animals living like themselves.'

6th – The Bee Beard

Bee beards are temporary exhibitions. A swarm will cluster around a queen, even one kept in a cage in a person's mouth or under their chin. Records are kept by weight, since numbers are hard to count for boys who can't yet spell. Be our guest at the all-body bee pelt wedding.

All six – The Sacred Bee

Flowers open like hearts to receive ambassadors amidst the buzz of protocol – angels in priestly work attire. The cup may be full but never overflowing: a spill is the devil's mischief. Candles at mass are the bee's pledge, exhaustion of the soul in service. The hive will never die.

12

THE GAME

'As God is my witness, if you pick up the second King of Spades you can't then remarry the Queen! Ask the Tsarina if you don't believe me.'

The opening ceremony is the dedication of objects; the closing ceremony is the thump and yelp of a silverback, probably neutered. No compromise is brooked: you can be in or out but not somewhere between. Inattention explains the black market in lost pieces, though many are stolen. Losers may resort to sabotage, a virulent flu strain amok in the house of cards.

1st – The Ancient Game
In the wreaths of the dawn on a wild young planet, stones are chinked beside the campfire's roasting boar. There's time before carving, since drinking leaves hands free for minutes on end. Later, even wars will be delayed, funerals brought forward. Funerary games are the fiercest of all.

2nd – The Romantic Game
The parsonage constrains, but if the wind off the tops is allowed its truancy, let fancy follow suit. For their brother's toy soldiers the girls make up stories, educating his African confederacy, bringing sentiments to settlers. 'Alone I sat the summer's day.' 'I'll come when thou art saddest.'

3rd – The Solitary Game

The singleton tends to win against time but to lose against destiny. His blinkers are set to matches and sequences, numbers without arithmetic, courts without histories. Ignoring bargains and beckonings, he wins repeatedly, the triumph of closure, humourless in the cave of his animation.

4th – The Therapeutic Game

Domino skills are resilient. Bright as a pip, he shuffles the boneyard of loose tiles on the table. It's carnival – tea isn't served but it's lively. This *dominus* is no French priest with a black-and-white hood – only an ancient mariner, kindly, slightly trained, and lucky to have all his marbles.

5th – The Diplomatic Game

Wives defer to a men's game that starts after lunch and stretches into the slow decline of empire, the longest shadows. Intelligence is poisoned; there's whispering by the Moorish steps. Assassins bounce off the laurels. Betrayals rustle. Husbands bandage hurt feelings under cover of night.

6th – The Numbers Game

The cavernous Essoldo is echoing with numbers. Rags of threadbare language polish the engine of luck (since the thing is so noisy and slow). Donate your prize to charity – a set of personalised charms to clip on wine-glass stems. The national game foreshadows the worldwide web.

All six – The Operatic Game

Every melodrama has its sideshow. The duke keeps a chess set in his box, so close to the stage he can kiss the prima donna. The prodigy has never, until now, seen Verdi's *Macbeth*. He follows the opera while routing his competent opponents, the duke and the count, with a queen sacrifice.

13

THE KITCHEN

*'The kitchen-garage with a hubby hatch: this is now a must-have conversion
in the suburbs of the redwood dream.'*

The concept of wholesome living was the brainchild of a US architect
elusive in the annals. In her spacious domain the triple goddess animates
the frieze around her altar: cultured home cook, with giant spaghetti
towers; archivist of the husband's battle songs, the bubbling myth
cauldron; observant shepherdess of wolverines with winning ways.

1st – **The Troubadour's Kitchen**
A propeller in the chimney turns the spit, as if Leonardo had paid a visit
in the dead of night. Smoke rises around the hood, warming the solar and
driving vermin from the woodwork. While servants stir the broth and
polish the silver, cousins upstairs enjoy another hilarious dulcimer lesson.

2nd – **The Kitchen Sink**
Shrill accusations. An angry iron scorches a shirt, a pressure cooker flies
and crashes, waking up baby. Then the broom handle on the underside
of the floor, and two or three seconds of silence – all but the palliative
wireless voice like soapsuds from 'a factory somewhere in England'.

3rd – The Collector's Kitchen

Vegas is the mecca for magnets: every hotel has a treasure trove, often filling half the souvenir shop – overpriced, of course. Back home you consider bribing your mother-in-law to slip a few bucks to the senior housing super for any refrigerator gems going begging in vacated units.

4th – The Kitchenette

Caravan living: adventures in a portable landscape. The silent song of the bonny suds, technically Scottish, akin to the firth's foam, their rainbow a fractal of the marvels over Suilven, lochans sparkling after rain in cleansed sunlight. Chores are so light and fleeting in the mountains.

5th – The Rustic Kitchen

An abused gas Aga costs a thousand pounds for a proper service. All you can do is waitress at more farmhouse weddings or pressure-wash more chicken sheds, meanwhile making do on the electric hob donated by the gas-safe engineer who divined a leak on the scary side of the floor slates.

6th – The Extended Kitchen

Green fingers gallop in retreat from the culinary onslaught. Recession has loosened red tape, leaving the south-side neighbours defenceless. You gift them, via amazon, a starter pack of shade-loving seeds: Pansies, Yellow loosestrife, False lupine, Virginia bluebells, Canada columbine.

All six – The Kitchen of the Seventh Happiness

What is the sound of no tap dripping? The toaster's crumbs evacuate into the compost shoot. Like a shaman, acid-cool, silkily the knife skills graduate glides into his sacred arena. There's one anomaly: a timer in the form of a leaf-hatted votary in the temple of the Dragon of Peace.

14

THE ISLAND

'No sense of an overcrowded nation at your back as you stand on the shore, gazing at the sea's horizon: only the love of a continent.'

A private island you can walk around in a morning has come onto the market. One tree is a famous visiting book. See the earrings screwed into the bark? – that one was Taylor's. The beach cave is a movie theatre, air-conditioned. Scallop shells in the boathouse conceal speakers: the ocean was recorded at Clint's place in Carmel, four thousand miles away.

1st – The Island on the Ring of Fire
The plate is pushed over a hotspot in the mantle beneath – an upwelling plume of magma where a volcanic island flowers, reaching up to air from the ocean floor, a marine lotus, entertaining new flora and fauna. Then off it slinks, usurped by a younger sibling right over the stable melt source.

2nd – The Island Indoors
Rum punches are handed out to the audience. The plantation owner binds his daughter with tarantula yarn. The black slave, cutting cane, resents the whole colonial catastrophe. Prophetic strange fruit hangs in the brief twilight. Ariel flies down the centre aisle, exulting in the mind's freedom.

3rd – The Prison Island

Waves are playful in the bay of storms. A cell phone is akin to a conch, an attribute of power secreted in one's fundament. A pirate was shipped in, prompting hilarity: a hoarder of britcoins, buccaneering in cyberspace. Self-help is obvious: imagine yourself on a ship or a flight to the stars.

4th – The Sinking Island

All the parrots are in aviaries abroad now. The few mammals have a hangdog look, as if they smelled the coming inundation. Among them are a dozen skinny cows, and each one has a name, a charm against loss. In this place of apparatus every catamaran has a net of fine mesh amidships.

5th – The Rock Island

Music rattles the mainland – promenade guesthouse bedrooms. Fans who can't be squeezed into the field moan into their mobiles. Fireworks over water image a guitar. Interviewed in the telly tent, the professor hypes his new history – locals buying guns, Morrissey signed up at a boat show.

6th – The Invisible Island

Although herring gulls' calls evoke the wrong hemisphere, the sleepy lagoon is as blue as the Führer's eyes. Our presenter is defensively shifty – too many recent guests are from his native Illyria. The grand piano is totally taboo: it might be used for shelter. Luxury? A six-way mirror.

All six – The Island of Rest

In a nondescript vessel for the train, her ashes are stolen by a junkie who mistakes them for cocaine. They were meant to nurture roses on Tresco. The daughter browses shelves in a retail hangar. Tresco's head gardener no doubt has potash; but she needs it *now*, for comfort on her trip.

15

THE MOTHER

'She copes with the phase of obedient moments, extending by a short renewable lease the longevity of everything breakable.'

When she leaves the room for breastfeeding, the committee carries on voting. In the chamber one problem is the 'behaviour of honourable members'. The sergeant-at-arms is conducting a comprehensive review. Meanwhile, as she deals with papers and committee work, the child is looked after in the chief whip's office, where he enjoys the bright décor.

1st – The Mother of the World
The 'v' in Eve is the primal curiosity, ushering in night, a blackness in mouth and heart. Animals turn predatory. Knowledge is curtains: part them to learn from Easy Street. She brings us drama – a sense of the irreversible, of lost footing after birth. And there she is to guide our steps.

2nd – The Mother Expecting Labour
Oh that insubordinate third baby! The vindaloo disappoints: bowel and uterus remain stalled. The midwife tries induction tricks – getting her to inflate balloons, climb up and down stairs; then membrane-sweeping, with circular finger strokes inside the cervix. The phone rings: 'Any joy?'

3rd – The Jubilant Mother

He battles a storm, out on a spar, changing a sail at midnight – youngest
of the crew and most at risk. She drives thirty miles to the coastguard
radio. 'You've got a distinction!' Embarrassed monosyllables, no mention
of herself, reassure, like a halo of light and strangers' shouts in the fog.

4th – The Mother's Rules

Don't speak if you've nothing nice to say. Avoid bad words like 'stupid'
(though some allow swearing if it's not *at* anyone). Don't play with
cutlery or food. Befriend the friendless. Mistrust popularity. Set a spider's
loom on a clothes horse: observe who holds their breath.

5th – The Mother-in-law

Life lesions: her operation is tomorrow. The vortex of family feelings
allows no truancy. Every relationship is strained. Somehow you're
snagging, despite yourself, the net of sympathy. Idly you pick up a
catalogue of silicone breast forms, then drop it on the sofa in shock.

6th – The Prospective Mother

One broker scouts the reservations. She imagines high cheek bones,
tracking skills winning friends at school, the mystique of blockish
language. There's a minimum age of resale: think how the child might feel
about that delayed gold bridge, the cruise brochure on the doormat.

All six – The Grandmother

Humbug-striped, the woolly hat and double helping of sweaters bring
a light sagacity to the links. A boisterous wind blusters. Grandchildren
squeal, as if in a railway tunnel. But the truth is, she has smothered her
drive. She smiles and does her little stomping mime of exasperation.

16

THE HORSE

'A horse can unseat a prince and get away with it, so long as the prince is neither a child nor scared of his people.'

Never yet recorded, the closest secret is earthed when a rider dismounts: it retreats to the columbarium of mysteries. Two riders who meet in a hayloft may occasionally borrow that passion. Here is the food pass, the smuggled sugar lump, the muzzle's heartbreaking nudge. Brimming with poignant intelligence, the eye balances a tear on its melancholy shelf.

1st – The Dream Horse
Such was her yearning, she climbed through a hedge one day and leaped bareback onto a pony, which threw her. Her treasured charm, a gift from a groom, is a currycomb. Sometimes she'll flare out her nostrils, whinny, then jump over a log in the woods. 'Stroke my mane. Bring me apples.'

2nd – The Wild Horse
On the interminable steppes, from the Urals to Mongolia, horses are born of the lamenting wind. We conjure their ungainly grace, glimpsed in a brutal fondness. The feral sparks off the wild with the farrier's iron dedication. Wild peace is one of our most cherished and distant dreams.

3rd – The Fearless Horse

Swimming is prescribed for a horse over-fattened on grass. There's a
circular moat, the trainer on a small island. Nature is more extreme, with
terror a half-turn from the beach. Withers in foam show the mount heroic,
its rider more monstrous than the sea. War serves its baleful summons.

4th – The Pale Horse

All eyes are down for the rodeo of colour, the blessing in the litter of the
lost when a stallion mates with its daughters. The full chestnut paws the
ground; the weakling cremello weeps for its neural defects. And here's
the palomino, yellow and white, fated accident, gold coin of the parade.

5th – The Industrial Horse

Circus buyers swarm around horses in poverty, boys in tears. So much
is wrong with this paddock of the desperate auction. Don't imagine pit
ponies in sepia here. They were stabled underground, and only on certain
holidays blinked in the sun, the drunken village reeling all around.

6th – The Meat Horse

Wizards at their revels squeeze dung from intestines, to be stuffed with
fat and flesh – a yearling that baulked at its cab, a sadsack competing for
grain with men under siege. A tub of blood is left for the dogs. Such horse
magic has quit our shores – vanished on the hook or on the hoof.

All six – The Winged Horse

We're unlikely to succumb to privilege: unless entranced, we withhold
our love. The hero is a professional in a loincloth, bred for celestial polo.
His horse has inherited galaxies. At first, however, it refuses to fly. One
word, whispered in its ear, breaks down its resistance: 'Excelsior.'

17

THE GARDEN

'Tame your own lion with a rose-bramble whip. Its dung will frighten off deer from your flowerbeds; embolden your sweet peas.'

In the library of good earth the bindings are of muscle and sweat: the eternal apprenticeship. Unconsidered flyleaves are flags of faith – like the pages behind and ahead, seemingly inert. Study the seeding and sprouting, all that secret advocacy of soil and weather. Honour the endless editing, endless proofing; occasional flowering of pages in sun and rain.

1st – The Hydraulic Garden
On a sloping site like this she has to be cautious – she takes that whistling metal bird as a warning. In the garden of showery surprises, she practises her gracious shrug: what better remedy for sweltering Tuscan heat? The cardinal grins: God knows exactly whom to drench, this time at least.

2nd – The Therapeutic Garden
Life in the hands will flow back to the heart. Earthworms, millipedes, wood lice, beetles attend the granular sacrament. Like a mole you nose through your life's detritus. Anxieties let go; clichés wither on the vine. Whatever lands on your skin is all for the best in the weather of healing.

3rd – The Garden's Guardians

Salt will keep slugs at bay but mustn't be watered in next morning. You won't find toads for sale on market stalls any more, but toad men there are who'll ferret out your need, sweetening your plot with hymns of victory. Toad escapees from dogs and rats must be coaxed back into service.

4th – The Garden of Industrious Solitude

Cinquefoil, blackberries, johnsworth are a memory threatened by beans – seven folded miles, the oldest crying out for hoeing. Arrowheads point to exhaustion of nutrients by an extinct nation. Yet in this productive weed the yellow soil expresses its summer thoughts. Hardest is the selling.

5th – The Garden *sub judice*

A maverick of arbitrage votes for a lawn to replace uneven paviers – there's a wee one in the womb. A CCTV operative can wangle a discount to foil gnome snatchers. A pensioner hankers for a rare hebe, like a trophy for a life well lived. Indoors, animosities relax in their private gazebos.

6th – The Garden of Ill-gotten Gains

A third of all electricity theft is used to power these sweet-smelling indoor smallholdings. Sometimes there's a ordinary-looking bay with the TV on, the beds stretching back behind a partition. Look for a house in winter with no snow or frost, the warmth of guilt irradiating suburbia.

All six – The Imperial Garden

An emperor can be hard to surprise! The meteorite is slid on rollers in the sleeve of night, a gang of dumb illiterates negotiating the moon bridge. The caretaker lies drugged in the pavilion. The accomplice, hearing a horse's whinny and a rumble like thunder, smiles at her pillow book.

18

THE SECRET

"'Secret embarrassments are different from embarrassing secrets," explains the blush therapist with a reassuring smile.'

Secrets are among our impurities, the logic of experience crookedly unfolded at our feet. Once told, they can lash the soul with broken chains: is it better to live with the shackles? A lie may be a trial run: if it fails to come back as hearsay, your new friend is probably trustworthy. A patent is a secret first withheld, then shamelessly advertised.

1st – The Emerald Secret
This is three-quarters of philosophy. Ascending from earth, born of the wind, unwrapping light, flows the subtlest fire of the path those mercurial tricksters walked. Imagine a farm intensely enough: its fields will one day bleat and moo. Inhabit the brand: you'll dine every evening on a couch.

2nd – The Secret Restored
Digital photography thrives in bedrooms. Gifting the camera to your dear aunt was risky: what if she loses images and downloads software to restore them? Are your own unthinkable pictures safely in oblivion? You warn her on the phone: there are viruses thoughtless salvage may unleash.

3rd – The Secret Sorrow

Big, loud, wild events spark and crackle with harms. It looks and sounds like coldness: it's sadness. Regret for what *might* have happened or might yet, imagined chaos or catastrophe. It's the ministry of making do, of carrying on, the effort and shame of bringing empties to the bottle party.

4th – The Secret Sharer

Imaginary friends are never plural: there's a space problem. Company is the tango of souls, one of them dancing without footprints. A quiet passenger during your rampage in the hen coop, she audits the damage, self-employed, plumbing your moods, relaxed between invisible ears.

5th – The Secret Integration

Like the classmate who bakes cupcakes for his sister, trainspotters make plain sense of the world – what's not to like? There are awesome trains with hobo cabooses and spy chases flattening themselves for the tunnels. Commit to dynamic friendship: character jokes, the uncontested dowry.

6th – The Secret Love

She insists he desert his regular soap for her own family brand. So the husband is olfactorily superior? Silent synaesthete in bed? Could the roots of this love be hyposmia – nasal polyps, hay fever – nurturing her compassion? Bath time is a sweet goodbye – the return to echoey ego.

All six – The Secret Room

Touch the Field Marshal's eyeglass in the crusty old painting. A sanctum opens like a smile, ranks of classics juddering aside, a contraption at the end of its remit. Here a veteran grapples with marriage: 'Leave an outlet free when surrounding an army. Never press a desperate foe too hard.'

19

THE EGG

'*Two rookie questions: How does one candle reptile's eggs? And what if the neonate is pipped but just won't leave the shell?*'

A parameter is needed to calculate the parameter. Yet a proto-chicken's egg contains the embryo of the first chicken. This is the way to keep the question small, not using it to loose a large and heavy one. Brahmanda gives rise to the earth from its yolk, the sky from its white; or vice versa. Thoth either *hatches* the cosmic egg or else *emerges from* the cosmic egg.

1st – The Egg and the Berry
An egg, classified as meat in the American food triangle, is the antithesis of a berry. Plants have engineered the ultimate incentive to consume, a supernutrient package prolonging dispersal. The egg is an evolutionary expedient, risking dependency and predation for the sake of a quiet birth.

2nd – The Egg Hunt
The bomb squad invented it: an Easter egg emitting beeps that make the egg hunt feasible for the visually impaired. Once found, big on the lawn, it's disconnected by a volunteer, replaced by its reward, a traditional plastic egg filled with sweets, then reset for another child's enjoyment.

3rd – The Contraband Egg

Six peregrines released in Scotland have an exotic prenatal history,
escaping a predator caught at Dubai airport with fourteen eggs in socks
taped to his chest. They were chicken eggs, he insisted, for relief of his
back – swollen by rheumatic highland rains, twisted by a fall from a crag.

4th – The Sea Turtle's Egg

On a dark beach backed by woods without bars the drugs trade conjoins
with the poaching of sea turtle's eggs. An addict might even use eggs as
currency for cocaine. *Hueveros*, expecting to dig up several nests, instead
spy from the trees on an eco medic moving clutches to a secret hatchery.

5th – The Counterfeit Egg

Ruthless in its arms race, the cuckoo, in hawk-like plumage, lays a
mimetic egg. The warbler, freed from shame by lack of an imprint clause,
tirelessly feeds the giant imposter. Otherwise, having colluded with the
devil under a one-time curse, might it not shun its second brood?

6th – The Free-range Egg

This quota of hens per acre creates a grassless manure bath. Europe's way
is to place waterers and feeders deep inside a few small doors. Two or
three model hens peck outside. In a confinement flock surrounded by a
lawn trimmed beaks deter cannibalism. Yolks are suspiciously yellow.

All six – The Inconceivable Egg

The dove, symbolic imago, is seldom imagined hatching – though the
female is broody, purring, sometimes even loving. Like Venus it emerges
fully formed, enfolding our curiosity in its wings. It's lonely in its flight
but never vulnerable. The egg is too narrow an auspice for a race's destiny.

20

THE BRIDGE

'Though their faith requires slenderness, transparency for the landscape, there's an issue all bridge-makers face: the curse of the signature.'

Stresses hold their balance for the leap from shore to shore. Those who wish to linger often reduce themselves to some special provision, an eddy in the flow. Minutes are precious but an hour feels like forever. Most of us just dash across the word-break. So easy to miss the garrulous gist of an oarsman shooting for freedom, downstream from the slave states.

1st – The Bridge of Time
The school prodigy takes her friend to the bridge in the old town to show her the foam streaming back from the piers, proving the spin of the earth. 'Isn't it just the river flowing by?' 'What do you think the river is but the wake of our disappointments, which time, thank God, outpaces?'

2nd – The Bridge of Sighs
The rain comes down and the dark clouds frown. Howling big wind. A train rattles between high girders, cotters loose on chattering ties: shock loading on lugs under stress. In the dusky moonlight, northbound, we're relieved of our tickets. Then a surge of fear: we rise like a hot air balloon.

3rd – The Bridge of Missed Opportunity

Purposeful locals building with bamboo were never advised of the explosion plot. You're led to the site by a child extra, now a dishevelled, importunate tourist guide. Here are shallows with a few might-have-been concrete abutments – elusive stumps in the mouth of the dream horse.

4th – The Bridge of Spies

On one side the spy plane pilot, who should have jumped without his parachute to avoid capture; on the other, a codebreaker with a headful of chess. Months of back-channel ploys converge. Bundled in dark overcoats, they trudge across the bridge in a snow dome of overlapping searchlights.

5th – The Sheltering Bridge

Sleeping under arches, this clan might hope at best for the river's surprises – floating fruit, a charity boat plying its improbable mission. Their children, however, believe in the *gendarme* deranged by a lottery windfall, grinning weirdly, unlocking the street cells, waiving the camping bribes.

6th – The Bridge of No Return

A scaffold so high above water offers a quick, reliable result for a month of planning. Forcing the lock, the father finds a bookmarked website for jumpers; then gets a call from the highways office an ocean and a continent away. A village hears its baffled anger boiling in the pulpit.

All six – The Bridge of Heaven on Earth

Architects, bankers and City Hall supremos mingle at a Freemasonic dinner on the theme of Wings and the River. Behold the first stirrings of the harp, the celestial steel. Beneath the moment's vault, the flow of eternity, a rippling curveship in the smog storm, anchored in granite.

21

THE HERMIT

'Music for the hermit. Unlike heat and light, this is a gift he'll struggle to refuse, sitting in a grotto in his busker's cap.'

He calls himself Coyote. Of his thousand burglaries he is proudest of those that might be attributed to forgetfulness – a book lent to a neighbour, a half-eaten loaf fed to the birds. Children also make good suspects. A note is nailed to the porch door: 'Please don't break in. Write down what you want and I'll leave it out for you.' That would be a relationship surely?

1st – The Hermit's Cousin
His holt is a childhood den, known to the old gang. Sandwiches are left in greaseproof envelopes with a get-well message– a summer cold has been heard. For his birthday, a classic study of the Picturesque – a relief: he feared a surprise party in the copse, candles dripping among the pines.

2nd – The Hermit in Love
Rocks are for flinging into a gorge, trees for dismembering. Wild nature has exploded out of paroxysms of desire. Your challenge is to invite a lady to your lair. This prospect appals. The secret? Listen to the wolves that reared you. Ignore your fair-weather friend, the nightingale.

3rd – The Republican Hermit

Disarmed of spikes by munitions men, this is the easiest of parks to trespass in. That camp on the single islet of the lake, unfairly described as 'foul' by a diarist, is where the skeleton was found, a vodka bottle tied around the neck – escritoire of all those angry letters to the Queen.

4th – The Would-be Hermit

Face muscles flinch defensively like a bush in a storm. The big outdoors gets caught in the eyes in meetings. Occasions are alien. Yet the bank would open its doors to a tree sprite with savings, a crossword-solving brain in caddis-case camouflage. This is the leniency she seeks to escape.

5th – The Rainforest Hermit

A lone survivor in a narrowing tribal cul de sac, he hunts and dreams at the safe end of a thirty-mile radius of immunity. One rescue worker died from an arrow in the chest: the tribesman was pardoned. The no-trespass ruling is strictly enforced. His native aura holds back waves of logging.

6th – The Robotic Hermit

He's dented from the fall – some of the tree roots would be taller than his stride. Control overrides his arms and legs, switching from auto to program. Hopeless! And the neck fails to articulate – the gearing's gone. Vision is frozen: blizzard of falling leaves; conkers like asteroids.

All six – The Hermit Scholar

The beard's zoography is an omnishambles, an ecosystem spreading, yet thoroughly systematised. He is the midwife of rare births, the lengthwise witness – at right angles to the stars. Trespassers are welcome, even predators if they dare, and know their place on the terrestrial food ladder.

22

THE MOUTH

'A highlight of the first International Phonetics Symposium will be a click song in Ndebele — with drum accompaniment (tsk! tsk!).'

Mouth breathing, speaking of the private troubles of the nose, shows symptoms akin to vacancy. Yogis find the practice disgusting. Exhalation through the broad hatch of the mouth reduces back pressure, hastening air escape, giving the lungs a shorter shift. When smallpox decimated men-of-war on distant seas, not one nostril-breathing sailor succumbed.

1st — The Mindful Mouth
At rest you feel the press of a chair, a light confiding touch of shoes and socks, sleeve ends, collar ridge, trouser knees, but most meaningfully the tongue in its gently lapping boathouse of the same conscious stirring, endlessly ready for the voyage of a lifetime, without ever leaving home.

2nd — The Unconsoled Mouth
'Never' means 'unacceptably seldom' to a partner driven to the edge. 'A domestic,' they say. 'We're the wrong kind of specialist.' But uniforms do bring a temporary silence, blue-black vacuum of night beyond the city. The mouth is innocent, save in trespassing on the ear's thoroughfares.

3rd – The Mouth's Cry for Help

Closed mouth while speaking: a soundalike for a revered warrior's name, this is our portal for guidance from the silent therapist. Still so far away, the estuary of the glottal stop. In later life she'll write to an agony aunt: 'I hate it when guys especially look at your mouth while you're talking.'

4th – The Mouth of the World

A chemistry-set cuvée sucks: the *terroir* was probably a speedway track. An oaky contender gives you a mouth full of splinters. There's a fruit bomb too, crass and slutty. The epiphany is a critter wine, Madagascan! Redolent of vanilla, cinnamon, baobab smoke. Label: ring-tailed lemur.

5th – The Reconstructed Mouth

The gates of titanium, alongside old gold, make the temple of self and speech distinctive. Rituals are adapted. The mangled tongue finds its own resurrection, zombie-like at first, then naturalising – cunnilingus, to his relief, still possible. The trick is to ignore the constant reminders.

6th – The Meeting of Mouths

Two human resources managers, attracted, sifting cvs, launch themselves into the pink macro blur all of a sudden – the breakthrough escape from a gaze, a raid on the sweet taste of the other. Then, pulling back, briefly they study the improbable moon they've visited, back in its accustomed orbit.

All six – The Mouth of Truth

'Say what she longs to hear. If it's untrue I'll bite your hand off.' Thus threatens the upended Roman drain cover, wrought as open-mouthed Oceanus impersonating the god of the Tiber. Jilted soldiers make better fighters. A recruiting sergeant crouches behind the disc with a love letter.

23

THE JOURNEY

'You're still planning your reckless adventure, pondering what you'll need?
Just take half the clothes and twice the money, and go.'

He has a key but no door now: the airport needed a buffer zone. After
the boat, should he try train or car? Paid up front, would the driver show
up? Better to risk the timetable's hieroglyphics. Native newspapers serve
as your passport. On the cover of *Charlie Hebdo* Kate Winslet rises like
Aphrodite from a boat packed with migrants: '*Un Titanic par semaine.*'

1st — The Delayed Journey
Behind the station are two small public gardens — hopeful bosky
depositories for anyone travelling with a dog. Stalled in your circuit you
miss train after train, mocked by whistles in the steam. The lilt and tang
of your curses prompt sudden friendship among silent drifts of blossom.

2nd — The Hazardous Journey
The technician who prepped the engine normally works on motorbikes
and mopeds. Our souls, in their sky-rush, just clear the corrie's rim, the
volcano below us streaming with wrathful lava. Our pilot, crack batsman
of the upper school, paid in rare autographs, is contagiously gung ho.

3rd – The Journey of Dutiful Compassion

This mercy trip is a holiday in a handcart, the gift of a pineapple from
the oasis of well-being – as if a doctor had asked you to sit still for your
own good. A luxury free of guilt protects against sandstorms. You can buy
camels on arrival if you need them: for now you just drive, unshaven.

4th – The Journey in Winter

Snowflakes flurry and accumulate, as if flung onto graves from an angel's
shovel. This reminds the kids of angel wings, so in a lay-by we allow them
their heart-breaking *frottage* of innocence, willing the whole crew north –
though what we really need is grit some devil's grudge withholds.

5th – The Assisted Journey

The planet is mapped and the maps refreshed by their users – a karmic
system, saving us hours we might have spent peering at roads rubbed out
by folds and swivelling flapping sheets in cramped capsules. We boldly go
to the lighthouse – driving across sands, breasting the rising tide.

6th – The Long Journey Homewards

There's a bus stop and bench (a German innovation) and at the bright end
of homecoming an unlocked wardrobe. Packing takes many more hours
than waiting – most of the refugees are soon distracted, tricked back into
the lounge for a cup of tea. The general strike ends tomorrow.

All six – The Sacred Journey

Nodding wheat-ears hosannah pilgrims on mules, whose tall tales are
rumbustiously secular. At night they spill their souls in whispers. Given
the pliability of the medium, why has the revered face of the shroud never
flattened itself into a cornfield? Why all those sacred geometry clichés?

24

THE WELL

'Look, a woman at the well in the noonday sun! The other villagers must hate her, no doubt for immorality.'

Big glacial stones underneath might prohibit driving a point in the yard. A driven point seeks its own course: it would either wallop into a boulder and stop dead or else bend till the drive pipe broke or friction prevented further progress. A bent pipe, in any case, makes it impossible to install a suction pump. Many wells need to be drilled, and to hell with the outlay.

1st – The Well of Sufficiency

Enough of survival is tautology – erratic rains, crops, food, comfort. Abundance we give back for this. Our overlapping petals, like tiles on a roof, dress six wells in memory of lost cattle, burnt corn and hay, with thanks for fatigued resilience: our undaunted Bethlehem of births.

2nd – The Well of Purity

Any water looks special in an *auteur* bottle. The sociable inspector lingers over his *meze*. Down in the cellar loyal artisans pump filtered, carbonated tap water into flagons with engraved armorial cartouches. Municipal quality standards justify certification; even, just possibly, acclaim.

3rd – The Well of Loneliness

That distant hole of sky is choked with pitch – a locus: mere geometry. Friends will have their own monoculars. A conversation about the view could never *change* the view. Self-evident? Only if you lack the strength to learn about a working well, purer, somewhere in some nearby village.

4th – The Well on the Western Front

Conceding energy to mapping minds, the land between trenches reverts to abstraction. Yet in no man's land, where a broken well is choked with weeds, infantrymen see tiny parachutes floating between drifting clouds of dust and smoke, a telegram: there might be water still at the bottom.

5th – The Closed Well

Self-help culture has crept from the page to the big outdoors: *Discover; Enjoy; Imagine* – you have to, since the ancient well is closed, a grassy throat of earth with a plank across its mouth. An old-timer knows better: 'How can you close a well – even in our bankrupt Age of Aquarius?'

6th – The Well of Gravity

A fragment of a planet, goddess of sight and the earthly sky, which collided with earth to create the moon, sits at rest in its space pocket. Likewise, her engagement ring, thrown into a well, has nowhere else to go, its rare glint of moonlight not seen by a soul, eternally unpromising.

All six – The Wishing Well

A coin is best, though a letter might work: it has to be something that might have enriched you a little. From that loss you draw the energy of luck, rubbing until it shines like an affirmation. Think of your wish, not as a souvenir from a place you'll never visit, but as a first instalment.

25

THE LEADER

'Creatively leverage the passion of your Tao self-branding. Run your followers delicately, as if cooking tiny fish.'

A kingfisher in the gloaming is the only signatory to a compromise hammered out on a duck punt. Back home there's a kill list, encrypted; drones patrol his dreams. The native quotas are unattainable without patrician support. Loathing meetings, where there's no place for the mellow, he relishes decanter politics, glimpses of tradition, of children.

1st – The Liberating Leader
The helmsman's next obsession is the sparrows: if every peasant bangs pots and pans they'll fall out of the sky, exhausted. True, grain is saved, but the cost is huge: relieved of predators, locusts descend and strip the land of strength and skill, while he orchestrates the war of the bedbugs.

2nd – The Humble Leader
In hand-me-down brogues she treads the cobbles of moorland mill towns, handing out leaflets, smiling. Elected, she surrounds herself with a coterie of potmen, lamplighters and dinner ladies. She foresees the end times, the blaze of her father's books, and border people turned into gibbons.

3rd – The Leader in Exile

Charisma grows in silence at the unofficial heart of the nation – a train
running clockwise inside the frontier. Mail is redacted, gifts dismantled.
One day we see skywriting: a voter's cross, dispersing back into the blue.
Celestial birthmark. Wavelets of courage ripple across the rice fields.

4th – The Leader at Bedtime

Raised eyebrows are televisual, but not this outrageous hamming
magnified by marriage. Undressing always brings out the mischief in
him, with an unparliamentary audience of one. Their intimacy makes him
funnier: the comedian trapped in the fridge, thriving on inconvenience.

5th – The Leader's Statue

A painted statue oiled as a bowling pin stands erect, like a warning model
build a stone's throw from a school – but giant-sized, to match the people's
pride in their bountiful leader. His thousand-room hotel in the new
capital, monolithic, not yet populated, ruthlessly practises its welcome.

6th – The Eloquent Leader

Advertising seduces and the glister rubs off – you should hear the talk in
the mewsier pubs of Mayfair and the estuarine laxity of Number Ten sofa
meetings with the spin circle. Sincerity is a social skill, a thermal on which
to fly highest – a soaring hawk, bringing peace to the world's naïveté.

All six – The Spiritual Leader

His surgeries, though codified, are never copied, since ink is no juice of
the desert. His mind is a case of scalpels, materialised out of a cloud on
Ararat. The seers of the heart are long occluded, yet he with the fan-like
beard knows the truth by its word, which is all humankind can endure.

26

THE OWL

'The call from tree to tree makes total sense of the darkness. The wood just woke me when it drained itself of light — you too!'

They venture from their lairs, a furtive demolition crew. Daylight, not this dark, is the realm of secrets. The woodland floor is teeming — careless around the base of the food ladder. Above, on a branch: a booby-trap of eyes and claws, patiently still on its fuse of ruthless hunger, crouched within its eyebrows. Its left ear, pointed down, picks up pattering raindrops.

1st — The Owl of Unquenchable Desire
Mother turns Daughter into an owl, enticing her up a tree and making her flap her arms with a loud *hoo hoo* till she takes to the air, leaving her skin behind — disguise to snare soft Son-in-law on talons of flesh. Her eyes dilate to see his innocent scampering soul as he drinks elemental earth.

2nd — The Owl Journal
Pellets are broken like bread, their random slices studied like a miniature Torah, unfolding intricate exhibits of the tundra — a clavicle or two, a mandible with molars and incisors, skulls of voles and partial skulls of lemmings. Beware: this is the ancestral home of the clothes moth.

3rd – The Owl Count Competition

A hire car trundles on what's little more than a goat track. Inside, tired young minds are diverted by the spotting challenge. So far neither Sunita nor Dexter has noticed the upslope distribution of broken-down farms, and therefore feathered finials, in this godforsaken outpost of Athene.

4th – The Owl of Union

On the threshold of the house of the usher, the falconer flies both rings, in a white feathery rush and contraction, onto the best man's gauntlet. Hooked into his sleeve, like a conjurer's folded dove, hangs the barn owl's consideration, seigneurial morsel, a juicy broken mouse.

5th – The Owl and the Parrot

All those second-hand signifiers! – the pirate of empirical truth despises heretical parrots. An owl sits silent on his shoulder's rat-tailed epaulette, a beacon of peace in ventriloquist Venice. Harlequin is ubiquitous here, echoing false blandishments and questioning the owl's earnest diplomas.

6th – The Eagle Owl

Oil platforms report no landings; fly-bys are unheard of too. Our forty or so pairs are no doubt kingly escapees that have teamed up on the run, sharing dark nights in cold caves, or the offspring thereof, putting time as well as space behind them, pluckily shuffling off their manacles.

All six – The Owl of the Baskervilles

Forget the homely hobbit's croft: sparing and nuanced, the short-eared margrave billows up from a silver-birch camp on the high moor, at the triangle where roads confer, eyes peering in complicity from cars, pale orange raiment, drifting in its noble office, effortlessly deflecting blame.

27

GOLD

'Be fortune's horseman, not its horse. Ride gold to the end of time's alley.
Sunbathing in splendour makes a fossil of us all.'

Money elopes to gold like the clothes peg infanta to her prince annually
enriched by meteor showers. Protected from poisons and revolution,
nevertheless he frets about downstairs rumours of social reconditioning
– crypto-utopian nightmare of gold cistern, manacles, ink and chamber
pots; the brass eagle lectern dripping with pondwater, gilded with scum.

1st – The Gold of Springtime
Spring rains reprise their tragic miracle: gold is the earth's new skin
before the green, requiring sacrifice, the victims flayed and priests dressed
in their hides, stained yellow in the manner of gold leaf and singing
hymns of praise. Seedlings prevail. The flayed god is the goldsmiths' god.

2nd – Gold and Silver
Silver envies beads running around like mice on the palm of the hand.
It's a light corsair, racing to strategic positions, mobbing the bullion hulk.
Its pricing is nimble and dangerous, up and down like mercury. Gold is
the fiat of calm, keeping us steady till nightfall, high on the silvery sea.

3rd – **The Gold Thread**

In a mountain gold rush village, prospectors, children of nature's desires
drunk on the promise of wealth, tease out their tiny bounty to a hair
threaded from hut to hut through open doors to disseminate their luck –
and weave a web to ensnare the great world's wandering widow.

4th – **Gold's Absence from the Upper World**

The rainbow's mission is to renovate the ordinary – while signposting the
vulgar carnal miracle. Treasure Island gleams only in the promise of its
sunrise. Spraying teasels should be outlawed and in some parishes may be.
Gold that never stays prompts whispers that procreate in the shadows.

5th – **The Gold Bullion**

The Higgs Boson heist is legendary. A wheezing Ford Transit rides
through the Kentish night, low on its suspension. The smelt boss, trapped
in a sting, learns the promise of Ecstasy in prison. The gangmeister buys a
rock star's mansion and two Rottweilers he names Higgs and Boson.

6th – **The Gold Medal**

Podium risk assessment is the new frontier of the sporting profession –
leaving aside performance. Victors mustn't bite too hard on their medals:
there's a slippery snake of copper as well as a quantum of silver. Comet
trails of ribbons are the tipster's pick for long-term gain and glory.

All six – **The Golden Fleece**

The Austrian pastoral cadaver is plumper than the Spanish. When
armour's worn, the badge may be engraved into the steel; sometimes
it's gilt. A heart of faith purges the memory of profligate pagan odysseys.
Onwards! This golden fleece is Gideon's, soaked in the dews of heaven.

28

THE SEA

'The kendai is a fake bluefin, a hatchery bum, with no more understanding of the sea than a concubine in the court of Genghis Khan.'

Pilots who ditch their planes and take to a life raft qualify *ipso facto* for the Goldfish Club. Crossing-the-line humiliation brings protection by order of King Neptune. Copies of certificates, for these and similar maritime decorations, sidestep the forces-wide supply systems. Rarely, a local command will make unofficial use of the regular print shop.

1st – The Sea Change
The tidal reach is the amphibian experiment, a marsh lab fermenting unattended in the moonlight. Study the documentary *Zone*, momentous like its prequels. Without currents to bring them morsels, terrestrial creatures learn to move their heads. They growl and stand their ground.

2nd – The Sea in Contention
The surf and the tide continue their uneasy dialogue in the stadium. In the green corner, prudentially checking pebbles in a prospector's pan: the care of the soul. In the blue corner: the doomsday machine, with its tactic-swallowing strategy, skilled at using the enemy as a weapon.

3rd – The Sea of Dreams

Wild years in Malibu: 'a way of life on the wave tops'. *Life* magazine's rubric rides fathoms over the soulful undertow, beguiling sociopaths surfing on breaking families, among California beach girls hating each others' hair as much as Maui surf girls love each others' hair, and comb it.

4th – The Sea Cure

Erectile problems crave healing foam: strip off, plunge in, for the closure of old wounds. The Baltic is perfect: an avatar of Venus, rising, would complicate matters. Tourist bars are suitably distant, their music drowned by contact calls of supplicants hitting the cold sea, genitalia retracting.

5th – The Sea Cave

Humankind against nature: this is the triumph of the species. The blow hole is the least of it. Musically, all agree, the show is a failure. But the spectacle is unprecedented, thanks to a genius lighting crew. Virtually all creatures here are stone-eating, imperceptibly enlarging their habitat.

6th – The Violated Sea

Solo yachtsmen fall prey to a melancholy deeper than separation. Please let this not be grief – imagine how you'd feel, discovering that you're sailing on the corpse of love, eerily free of scavengers, amid seabirds with full stomachs starved, drowning, victims of the sky god's condoms.

All six – The Sea of the Unconscious

We learn the truth at a round table in a land-locked country: minds are jellyfish on cosmic currents. Hence simultaneous invention, often taken for plagiarism. Logic today, *mana mañana*. Our words are either rock pools or icebergs. The night sea dive will take us to archaic wreckage.

29

THE CUPBOARD

'The mother needs rest. From the nurses' muster point you can see the stationery cupboard, door open. Baby lies asleep on a mattress of Jiffy bags.'

We seldom turn to look when hinges squeal. Discreetly accurate, they are mostly silent, even if lacking ball bearings. Complex things often outlive simple things – a panel of wood, a unicellular organism. Guileless creatures have the shortest span, whereas many who walk past cupboards lead long lives, never opening them, nor wondering what's inside.

1st – The Somnambulist's Cupboard
O world of jagged edges! Raised knives swing down in heartless radii. The golem stands rigid in his cupboard, like a missile, dream-controlled. Our sleuth finds only a dummy. The asylum holds further mysteries … but no body. The woman was so beautiful, he abducted her instead.

2nd – The Toy Cupboard
Blyton's dubious exotics endure house arrest on the top shelf. Still hard to reach are special toys like the Avengers set with Elan, Bentley, two avatars and three umbrellas; and the Predictor (friend to anti-aircraft fire) on three wobbly legs. On the lowest shelves are sundry bears of conflicted status.

3rd – The Political Cupboard

Sell-by dates are regularly patrolled: labels face outwards. One by-law is: be sorry when you've unwittingly bought a duplicate. Some know the half-lives of ginger, tapenade, capers; others peer and sniff. The final straw is that yellow patina on the shelf: a finger sweep decides the day.

4th – The Linen Cupboard

Since nurses are occupying all the rooms near Grandfather's, she sleeps for once in the domestic wing; and gets to see the renowned walk-in linen closet – a pantry for fabrics! Stains on percale sheets are faint as winter shadows – uncomplaining bruises of loyal industry, toiling at tradition.

5th – The Cupboard Where Trouble Starts

He's chatting to the client when water starts pouring out of the shower pump. Clipping pipes in the airing cupboard must have started vibrations. A piddly little washer was all that connected the hot/cold mix output with the pump assembly. It was all a brand-new gig – faulty out of the box!

6th – The Broom Cupboard

Carefree moments in the Mandarin Oriental: a chambermaid with a poker star, at play among her utensils. They leave singly, in an aura of dried disinfectant. It's embarrassing, walking into another cupboard, his glasses still in his case. The bellhop imagines him squinting at a royal flush.

All six – The Hideaway Cupboard

An elder sister with closed eyes is counting. By the time she reaches a hundred, he knows the place well, what movements he can make and what he can reliably lean on. Footsteps come near, recede, return. She lets in a flood of bullying light and laughter. Good morning, heartless Vienna!

30

THE HUNT

'If the trophy hunter fails to close with an animal that satisfies his strict criteria, he may never fire a shot all season, except, in the final weeks, for meat.'

The raffle prize? The chance to name and shoot a lion. He's licensed to take three and ship their heads back home. An English-speaking bearer comes with the package. Each has a multi-magazine rifle. Well-behaved children are welcome. Before the kill he frames a silent prayer, for his great-aunt's benevolence and his lovely ten-year-old daughter's aptitude.

1st – The Hunt for Wild Dogs

When wild dogs abounded, deer were seldom seen. River scrub was alive with songbirds. Now it's tall and green again, the birds are back in paradise, hoisting their filigree of brags and warnings. These dogs are the finer adversaries: deer carcasses make huntsmen feel like pest controllers.

2nd – The Huntsman's Letter

'The rich soil holds scent well, the quickset hedges offer no barrier to the competent, and there's a heavenly absence of wire, barbed or otherwise.' Next for his mother he describes his inaugural morning. An account of a good run, by one who can both ride and write, makes charming reading.

3rd — The Huntsman's Chariot

A maharaja has customised his Rolls-Royce Torpedo for tiger hunting.
Low-geared for stealth, quietly it creeps through the jungle. It has
mounted guns, spotlights for night hunting, and a safe with contingency
rupees for the family of any ground crew killed by a tiger or an elephant.

4th — The Hunting of the Herd

A stripping party at the cliff's foot waits for the fall — buffalo on buffalo,
lured by the running man with horns. Tongue, brains and liver are eaten at
once by a hungry tribe. Farther east, on the plains, horse-mounted hunters
ride alongside, shooting arrows, markers of ownership and prowess.

5th — The Man Hunt

It would be worth it even for a tithe of your haul: an escape app, with
GPS, pinpointing reliable rooftop leaps, the pipes used by frogs to cross
motorways, monasteries that ask no questions. Cut your own hair; or
stare at the barber till he looks away. Crawl. Let your accent pick up burrs.

6th — The Hunting Horn

An amateur whip, expected to hunt with mink hounds, finds blowing the
horn a tribulation. Some days he elicits a sound; other days he could cry.
The solution? The kiss of life for the embouchure. Keep a horn in the car:
practise in a traffic jam or at the lights. Avoid ornamental horns on eBay.

All six — The Hunt to Extinction

Shaggy hunters deride the animal extinction public apology initiative;
smooth townies conserve their prowess in a regulated wilderness. The
spearhead species will be the great auk, plucked of its feathers and left to
nature's will; or the quagga, beautiful zebra forequarters fading to horse.

31

THE POET

'Catch me some radio words, elegant on the page. Lucent. Patina. Cerulean.
Only a vibrissa from the indescribable essence.'

Your to-do list has two topics: the Chinese wheelbarrow, suggesting a
form; and 'Shenandoah', shanty of lost love, a thousand miles, oddly, from
the outlet mentioned. A ten-metre scroll of prosperous Suzhou shows not
one wheel, only sedans. A river or an Indian chief? Heartmelt flows down
not the intricate Yangtze, only the mighty Missouri, wide and rolling.

1st – The Poet's Apprenticeship
The academy is bright with next year's faces. The takeaway point from
workshop number one: 'A computer spreadsheet is efficient for checking
rhythm through column alignment. Transfer the text to a word processor
for fancier printing when you're done. (Check your sensory handles first.)'

2nd – The Poet Detained
The modernist project is the shaman's triumph. That word 'right' belongs
to a dangerous type of ambiguity. Tanks roll in with banners flying. The
renegade poet under house arrest is forced to be prolific, in notebooks
couriered every day by motorbike to the Museum of Social Achievement.

3rd – The Street Poet
In the Bairro Alto a lyric may reduce the price of irresistible comfort.
Many a streetwalker surfeited on flesh is happier to get acquainted with
the *ghost* of a machine pump juddering at full steam. With luck he'll
improvise on her loveliest particulars; if not, he'll probably pay more.

4th – The Elemental Poet
Social poets need not apply themselves; career poets ditto. Her roots are
gnarled homunculi, unrecognisable in a line-up; her leaves are *sui generis*.
A fraying tree is all nerves. Raptors tear across the spirit's wildness. Flat-
packers flounder: nobody believes the instructions any more.

5th – The Poet and the Printer
A call at 2am. He crawls out of bed in a blizzard of metaphor, scraping
ice off his car, driving on virgin snow. They are old friends who till now
haven't met. 'I must insist on the internal rhyme: assonance won't do!'
They trudge to the chicken yard, then check the pine marten traps.

6th –The Poet's Début
This Tibetan skull, silver-lined, with obsidian eyes, squats in the
bookshop, presiding over the launch. There's Thoth himself, signing
backwards without a mirror, a simian on his shoulder. A timid journalist
ventures, 'Would you call this your mascot, sir, or your totem?'

All six – The Poet in Residence
The rhymes for 'knit' are legion; ditto 'wear'. Her Walsingham is the
Immaculate Village where she browses the carousel of trolley tokens,
none of them embossed with her name: Maya. Her vocational wish list?
Moulin Rouge (Paris), Shard (London), International Space Station.

32

THE FOOTPRINT

'There are two extremes: the fresh print and the fossilised print; detection and preservation. Most of us escape both.'

Students stand in flour and then step aside onto paper. Meanwhile, the lecturer expounds one of the niceties of sleuthing: the marks of other non-living items (not just shoes). 'Think of bicycle tracks, or even a dinosaur's tail.' 'Correction, sir!' shouts one of the trainee detectives. 'It's now believed that dinosaurs leaned forwards with their tails in the air.'

1st – Footprints Underground

Touchdown, weight-lifting, kick-off: repeated millions of times. A few hundred bones are more elusive. A circle suggests a feast. A track may be a migration route or a shoreline. In the middle of a compact brontosaur herd are smaller prints, of youngsters protected by bulls or senior cows.

2nd – The Evidential Footprint

New studies flourish after the crime – history of chevroned sole or wavy heel, variations of a brand. Wet clay reveals not a limp but a slight list leftwards, a satchel carrier: schoolboy or courier. A round hole in the heel seems to implicate the former: is there a missing compass in the nettles?

3rd – Footprints on Water

Like improbable caring sex with a lonely neighbour recently widowed
(if the children cried, you'd hear them through the wall), it's little more
than the daytime trace of a dream. If you only half-believe, or even three-
quarters, that's far too little to walk dry-eyed through your vale of tears.

4th – The Yeti's Footprints

A shaggy man-beast pulls at dwarf rhododendrons. A male won't chase
you uphill: its prominent forehead will make you invisible. A female will
trip on her pendulous dugs. Strangely, snow tracks go from canine to
humanoid out of the shadows: sunlight turns wolf to yeti, werewolf-like.

5th – Friday's Footprint

We're taken to the level of the neuron, exploring the response of brain
cells to social events. The tropical beach is stamped by a rubber foot on a
long pole – much hilarity. Off camera, the subject swarms in unfilmable
complexity. Crusoe is in character, the professor in goat's clothing.

6th – The Contested Footprints

Dozens of amateur authors must have written the same thing. 'Where
two tracks in the desert become one, it isn't that you're alone: the Lord
has started carrying you.' An irresistible image reproduces as a meme, in a
storm of writs and polygraph sheets, as if scribbled by a hand in a cloud.

All six – The Bejewelled Footprint

Every time he steps on you, his tread leaves a footprint of jewels on your
skin. Although he's as heavy as an elephant, this footfall feels like a feather,
with a lesson for the ponderous heart: the weight of the world and its
sorrows remains so hard for us all to bear, even with tragedy lifted.

33

THE WHEEL

'The "wooden ox", the "gliding horse" flourish as ancient roads disintegrate.
The wheel takes all the load, the narrow felloe cleaving clayey soils.'

Oiling the hub are the three poisons: foolish pig, angry snake, uxorious dove. A potter shapes a dish, a monkey clutches at fruit, a swaddled corpse is left in the fetal posture to await the next birth. Directors, feeding on apples, and managers, tripping over roots, do endless battle. Orgies are planned for the library. Like flies in a jar we bounce and buzz.

1st – The Wheeled Armadillo
A Maya child, forbidden to watch the ball game, is pacified with a box of wheeled animals. Down the sloping lid she races a dog, a monkey, an armadillo, a puma. Skulls roll but delicate llamas do no heavy hauling. In a land without sledges and, as yet, no horses, the cart is still unknown.

2nd – The Wheels on Walker Mountain
Trekking uphill, they overtake a resting posse of cyclists; ten minutes later, hearing panting curses behind them, they make way to let them pass; soon they find them resting again ... and so it continues. Then the race down mountain fire roads, hub brakes burning the grease inside.

3rd – The Wheel of Law

A dynamic ex-farmhand installs a wheel in your lower abdomen. Turning smoothly, it cultivates your spirit, 24/7 – or, reversed, the spirits of all around you. The body evolves into a new kind of matter, able to fly to paradise. If each race has its own heaven, what of mixed-race children?

4th – The Wheel of Time

The atheism of cinema: two flimsy wheels – little more than pairs of flanges – obligingly carry their own lane, spooling *ex gratia* memories. Promptly the projectionist fixes breakdowns, at the ready on his roadside stool. Lovers at the drive-in check the rearview mirror for latecomers.

5th – The Reinvented Wheel

The Celtic cross is a survival manual: if collapse occurs we'll need to restart civilisation. A tragic occult history passes like a ley line through the burning of the Alexandrian library and the torture and execution of Templar leaders. Hub, hinges and spy holes qualify the tool for a patent.

6th – The Ferris Wheel

The Mets were losing to the Cubs when the stadium went dark. Our mayor was in one of the swing cars, sliding from rim to hub, with dignitaries from Beijing. Prior to rescue by manual cranking they could see only traffic's head and tail lights and the arsonists' first fires.

All six – The Stolen Wheels

The *magus rotarum* sports a bumper sticker: *Keep Suburbia Weird*. A few such beauties win converts in the showroom. All are compelling to drive – tactile, charismatic, no trace of iron Germanic. On four towers of bricks, the car signposts the couple's destiny: a belated return to the hearth.

34

THE ANGEL

'The angel in disguise at your table may ineptly face-paint your wee ones,
whose tears will mend holes in hand-me-downs.'

When the pharaoh in a jealous rage launched his genocide, the angel
who descended from Adam and from heaven led an army against him,
streaming like light from the sun in splendour. Though he'd dreamed of
desert nights warmed by angel down, soon he was praying for mercy.
Now his palace bears a sign: 'Beware: militant angels guard this property.'

1st – The Angel Explained

They roar like a lion or whisper like a lover. All the wings do is betoken
arrival from elsewhere. Rainbow scaling is a studio trademark. The body
weight-to-wing length ratio is wrong for gravity. You protest: the bones
are the divine plan, the flesh a Platonic idea, the organs a sacred rite.

2nd – The Angel Community

Their pinhead proves the medieval intuition of relativity. Space-time
is a bowl, whose outside surface we inhabit. Inside, all our deeds are
dropped, for reuse, easily picked up. Are we all alone when all is said and
done? Impossible to be sure while we're still so absorbed in dressmaking.

3rd – The Angel of Mortal Promise

There's a spectrum of thought, from earth-green dragons to the quizzical blue infinitudes. Allowed one wish, why not opt to become a bird-man parking cars to raise cash for flying lessons, while studying on steamy summer nights the quiet snowfall of small print, the pseudepigrapha?

4th – The Fallen Angels

'Akimbo' is the code name for the counterattack. There's a thrill in retribution, dropping them to an oubliette of the unimagined. You clutch at tumbling pinions, the day-long plummet towards the floor of the abyss where splattered serpents writhe. All possibilities remain unvanquished.

5th – The Angelic City

None has a taste for battle. Yet they see into the soul of the square mile, a nanosecond's trading edge, cruel fixes. Their war chest grows like wheat, a nursery for swords. Courage versus corruption: a system flawlessly working? Is bloodshed midge bites in the swamplands of Elysium?

6th – The Origami Angel

The paper engineer scoffs at your title: The Angel of the Vision Clinic. Yet he too was taking pupillage unawares, celestial energies doubled with every fold. This six-colour paper makes you think of Sainte-Chapelle. Heraldic litter storms dazzle the infidel camped in a rock-strewn valley.

All six – The Angels on Duty

How can eternals be clothed? Only from history's dressing-up box. The imperial bodyguard scintillates, Byzantine in his pallium; the angelic deacon gleams, stately in his cope and dalmatic. In a rush of swans' feathers down swoops the scribe – quill dripping basilisk's blood.

35

THE WHALE

'You've weathered homesickness, madness, pirates, scrimshaw, hellfire sermons. Time to drift placidly beside the pensioned leviathan.'

Incomparable mammals are losing themselves in the opacities of the blue-green *llanos*, the killing fields of contraptions not yet invented. A fascinated boy has nowhere to go, nowhere to start – unless he's lucky enough to have a whaling father, a benign one with a vision, inspiring tall tales of the deep, broadcasting the seeds of his dynasty upon the waters.

1st – The Whale Skeleton
A Gothic ribcage is the medieval godhead's masterpiece – unlike the human bone legacy collapsing on bequeathment. The fan vaulting is stupendous: connoisseurs are awestruck, while their children swing on the lower jaw. Yet the smallest vertebrae could be pilfered for marbles.

2nd – The Whale Museum
The crystal dome of the deep attracts thousands excited by the glazing – no ship-in-a-bottle subterfuge is possible with pickled flesh. Imperfect panes that catch blue sky simulate convincing waves. The glaziers keep their distance – all but one, who carves a harpooned heart under a fin.

3rd – The Pilot Whales

Reverse lemmings, one by one they strand themselves. Perhaps the first was sick, making for the shallows to avoid drowning; or else some solar or sonic anomaly jammed oceanic meridians. Go down the beach to them. Lever them side by side – the final consolation of fellowship.

4th – The Whale and Its Predators

Graceful matings in those endless dark vistas of space. The myth of the gentle giant: slowness and vast bulk, since there'd be nothing to escape were it not for harpoon history, the hungry pequods and the mechanised digestion of an industry afloat, the ego pitching camp on the common.

5th – The Whale of the Body Politic

Leviathan aspires to be a parliament, jaws on the surface propped open by statutes. Citizens electrify a benign animal passivity – prefiguring the giant Gulliver striding through Lincoln's streets closed to traffic, bringing the populace together in a carnival of misrule, a vaccine against anarchy.

6th – The Watchmaker's Whale

The surgeon was nowhere to be seen: the ships were lashed together, one captain seeking salves, or even surgery, for a harpoon wound. His watch was oiled by a fine, delicate fluid from the jaws of a bottle-nosed dolphin. But accidents happen. And memory can be unreliable, so far from land.

All six – The Musical Whale

In the calving grounds the humpback hangs upside-down as if on a butcher's hook, from its tail-fin anchor, voicing recycled air without vocal chords. His moans, growls and shrieks, caught with a hydrophone listening for submarines, breaks as a sonic tide on West Coast ashrams.

36

THE REFUGE

'Never pace the floor of a sanctuary; never mix past and future in the same thought; never dwell without intention on the undecided.'

Bullfrogs are croaking near the hut. Alder and poplar leaves are fluttering, yet the lake is merely rippled, not ruffled. Those who seldom visit the forest always steal some little piece of it to fiddle with as they walk. Drunk on country wine he sent the woodcutter's boy to fetch, he tosses off lines of wild calligraphy, in a script like trampled grasses.

1st — The Refuge from Time
A quotation from Pindar, in praise of water, embellishes the washstand. Olympian gods disport themselves on a glass shelf. Up to her neck in bubbles, she entertains an artist, a captain, a diplomat, all speaking well of the play, of her role as Rhine maiden, in youthful idioms on her birthday.

2nd — The Tornado Refuge
The twister wears a flying coat of greenish storm clouds. A passing construction truck stops by a trailer park: within the hour everybody sits in a shelter. Shingles, boards and satellite dishes fly by. A refrigerator is lifted out of a wrecked house, feathers are plucked from Tupelo chickens.

3rd – The Refugee Abroad

Pick up a banner without reading it. Click! Now you're the enemy. Her mother and daughter are still back home, without an embassy. She dreams of walking miles, dodging roadblocks. The Red Cross tracing service has lost its way. She tells her story, over and over – red thread back to Syria.

4th – The Refuge Crop

Ten percent of a refuge-in-a-bag crop will not be protected, unmodified plants suffering injury and yield loss. A separate corn borer refuge, rotated and treated with pesticides, is sited a quarter-mile to a half-mile from the modified field. Resistant and susceptible insects blithely mate.

5th – The Wildlife Refuge

Tourist murders make life riskier for mountain gorillas: deprived of visitors, hungry locals are drawn to the poaching gangs. This orphan a ranger carried through rain all day was found next to its mother shot in the head at close quarters, alongside a couple of bananas used to lure her.

6th – The Refuge from Suffering

Microprinting gives each prayer wheel millions of mantras. The Buddha of Compassion is manifest here and now, in the Pure Land. In your sickbed you may turn a wheel by pulling on a string. However, the merit of turning an *electric* prayer wheel goes largely to the electricity company.

All six – The Self-creating Refuge

Whole-body baptism of women required a 'deaconess' for propriety. Certain extravagant practices were condoned: 'widows' burning incense in the thurible, or anointing the sick. Widows and deaconesses were hard to tell apart. Certain rare transgressions came with their own sanctuary.

37

THE SHIP

'The whole crew is crowded into the crow's nest, scanning for Half-way Island. The leak is relatively small, so probably you'll get there.'

A cliff of portholes blocks your view at the end of a terraced street. Riveters migrate on other people's handiwork, then find their berth and fill the air with the blues. Rivet catchers hold out tin cans like the beggars they are not. Between the deafening creek of delivery and the wrecking shore deathbed, the pages of an iron-clad blockbuster turn on the tides.

1st – The Ship of Fools
On embarking you must look out for a man with a saxophone tie – the signal for the secret poker game. He'll slip a card into your pocket. An irregular holding pen for the soul, echoing like a gaol, squats behind a bulkhead. When the white cliffs loom you'll be penniless and free.

2nd – The Style Ship
A big-hearted film director is treating a bunch of pals to a steampunk orbit. Levers are the ultimate in retro-futurism; dials are cutting-edge. The colour scheme is fifties. There's a plush sofa. Even in blazing daylight some guests spend hours admiring their role models beamed out of old movies.

3rd – The Ship Aground

While the captain below jokes about property charts with his girlfriend, her brother, a maths student, commands the bridge. He has a friend in a writer's workshop in Ovid's crumbling house. Megaphone in hand, he steers so close to the shore they can recognise each other's beards.

4th – The Toy Ship

The salty old merchant seaman with Popeye on one bicep, Olive Oyl on the other, has Steiner teachers at his feet sharing manly plugs of chew. What a godsend to Cheltenham! It's summer, requiring a clever substitute for ice. In lordly self-delusion SS *Titanic* chugs among irascible swans.

5th – The Pirate Ship

Cringing is good for the soul: hence karaoke and pirate radio. Best of all is mock-heroic larks, as when a boatload of groupies arrive in branded T-shirts and filch the Jolly Roger. You need the anger room but there isn't one. There's no escape. You'd give anything for a plank, merciful sharks.

6th – The Wandering Ship

The geopolitics of the cruise, for some, revolves around the captain, their morning and evening star. In between, the souk, the pyramid, the tennis-ball minerals, the petrified forest – fragments gathered for his table. For others he's a small tax on free will, a stiffening of amply deserved leisure.

All six – The Ship Burial

The afterlife could never be a mainland, since our deepest longings require shores that do not slip sideways into foreignness. If the wind bends the smoke plume seaward, the gods may approve of our memory, love and honour rolled into one, and of him, with his thrall girl for company.

THE CRYSTAL

'Better to wear no gems at all than flawed stones. Better to make an enemy
of the tiger than a friend of the rat.'

Amethyst is a sponge for angst, animosity, arrogance. This is just one of
many crystals notable for their thirst. You desiccate around them, skin
patient for the moisturising kiss the virtuous will one day attract, filling
the vacuum left by a worn-out crystal. A new love blossoms on the lips,
the ordinary miracle in the jam jar of the self, the rusty nail beatified.

1st – The Crystal Wristwatch

The resonator makes the oscillator howl with the exact frequency required.
Quartz pulses are added or suppressed to offset the crystal's ageing. A twist
of the wrist will wind, not wobble, at work or play, in life off the level.
Motion and weather are no longer the enemy: only time and theft.

2nd – The Crystal Cave of Giants

A drugs honcho, in a vest insulated against frostbite, an ice vest on top,
and then an orange caving suit, his respirator pack blowing air over frozen
bottles, clambers among fallen obelisks of light – an extremophile in an
alien world. Smaller selenite crystals are fractured by his aura.

3rd – The Crystal Radio

One wire is clamped to the bedstead, the other pierces the veranda deck,
down to an underground pipe. Just above the eiderdown sits nirvana.
The slightest move jolts the whisker from its hotspot, losing precious revs
from the speedway over the river. The commentary, at best, is garbled.

4th – The Crystal Skull

Where was the finder at the dig? What has become of the log of the find?
The workshop sits by a worm hole in space-time. The receptionist's eyes
emit blue light. Atlanteans drop in and out in a nanosecond. An alert
ee-aws, announcing delivery of high-speed rotary tools from the future.

5th – The Canary Crystal

Mounted in a necklace of white diamonds, this yellow cushion-cut
brilliant with ninety facets was worn at the ball by a charwoman – a
misprint for 'chairwoman'. A sweep in Valhalla. Every diamond has its
prehistory of humble hands, grateful for all that light returned to the eye.

6th – The Crystal Initiate

They overnighted in soil. At dawn the Lemurian felt right, if a little strong.
Tiger's Eye (to a conservationist), Smoky Quartz (to a firebrand), Citrine
(to a birdwatcher), Amazonite (to a reader) were also irresistible – though
beginners should never buy too many at once: crystals can turn to tears.

All six – The Crystal Revelation

A clump of Pentagonite on a matrix grew ten flower clusters in a year.
Two of the blooms, half an inch apart, turned into one bigger cluster.
A third, once just a speck in a crevice, is now overflowing with needles.
Amazing! A home has neither heat nor elements for such formations.

39

THE SKY

'Passenger planes do not carry parachutes at present, since passengers are likely to object to wearing so bulky an object on a long flight.'

A water-powered armillary sphere engineered in brass foretells for learners and demonstrates for teachers the real motions of the earth, the apparent motions of the heavens. Rain fills the bowl – like myrrh to Arabia. Comets, eclipses affirm the imperial mandate – till astronomers, erring, lose their heads as the throne revolves into a new constellation.

1st – The Sky Parlour
The poet's room with a skylight is all civilised possibility, a promise both ways that needs only one signature. The pen, the notebook, can be of any style. Meteors occasionally cross the window by day but even at night are unnoticed – flaring potential, extinguished in the wink of its promise.

2nd – The Pragmatic Sky
Losing height above lion country, the balloonists debate their procedure. Youth, family, intellect, achievement, potential, all blow them this way and that. For a while there's a democracy, descending onto a dictatorship – without subjective will there's no consensus. Some at least are saved.

3rd – The Singing Sky
The song of the sky is incarnate in a lark, like an egg hatching in the warmth of a wish. Its only coordinates are self and sound, limited for sightings. Often you're the sole agent of a lucky capture, at large in the fenceless distances, a fluttery silhouette, yours for several seconds.

4th – The Fighting Sky
In the age of chivalry an enemy with a jammed gun or no ammunition was released from combat. Now strict rules are pinned up in the air base. Never fly straight and level too long, or fire too soon. Shoot out of the sun or the enemy's wing. Attack two-seaters from beneath their tails.

5th – The Sky of Royal Exile
The minister loyal to the exiled king is sacked for mumbo jumbo supporting a failed autocracy. 'Antisolar light streams through holes in clouds. That magnificent crown is an illusion. Those rays are almost parallel. Their apparent convergence is to the vanishing point at infinity.'

6th – The Sky Left Far Behind
A planetary gift must be more than a jar of jam, homemade or otherwise. Hence the golden record's murmurings – a monkey, a whale, the ocean, a baby crying, with thoughtful cartridge and needle. Languages from Akkadian to Wu: a Rossetta stone (naturally there's a common message).

All six – The Sky Burial
Where soils are thin, the sky is the deepest grave. Relatives chatter out of sight while the body-breakers follow their calling, pounding flesh and bones with tea, flour and butter, gossiping and making jokes. The vultures gather: the union in the skull cup is medicine, which can poison them.

40

THE MUSICIAN

'Even the most abysmal performance must be endured without anaesthetic,
since you need to be sure the nerves are still alive. Applause may be muted.'

Few instruments, even cheap ones, end up in landfill – far more in the attic's *parc fermé*, where superstition keeps them somnolent. Spiders float in strung lairs of trumpet, tambourine, accordion. The banjo – archetypal attic instrument – is reconfigured entirely. To play in such a house, in a living room or study, you must stop your ears to ambulance sirens.

1st – The Royal Musician
Pixie dust is no longer legal. While the old king in his finery bathes in the eternal concert of the spheres, his favourite composer slaves away at something suitably austere for the new broom's début. Let them pose for an hour of mathematics – the harp's revenge for severance of strings.

2nd – The Musician's Captivity
Jazz vocalists are all too often paraded for the family, devotees of the conservatory. Swing would smash windows. In a silvery mermaid dress she pitches her lieder, high on coloratura, oceans from Sugar Hill. The tragedy of the songbook, caged in a radio, tortured with floods of syrup.

3rd – The Musician Commemorated

In memoriam: the sitar player whom rock stars befriended, tempering their riffs, competing for a passive place on the platform. Appalled at the bonfire of guitars, he gravitated towards bluegrass – the whispering prairie, confiding its relaxed requiem for the long-time dead underfoot.

4th – The Musician in the Tunnel

The pressure wave from an approaching train threatens his pharaoh's high barnet. It's the customary Archway wind, anti-minstrel mistral, the Minotaur withstood with his fiddle valet. What's he doing here, far from the concert hall? Lost in the catacombs, he tosses change to a busker.

5th – The Bilingual Musician

The bilingual concert was a gesture of appeasement: naturally a riot broke out. The vocalist fled to a nearby love-in: the enlightened couple camping in bed, comforting this migrant petal, jamming, telling groupie jokes and dreaming up harmonies for voice and soapbox – all this in a hotel room.

6th – The Musician at Sea

Shoals of herring are off the playlist. Even so, there's a maritime mood: a girl on a moonlit shore. The smile, the kiss are a wildtrack of recollected youth, accompanied by fish knives and forks and a murmur of shipboard gossip over pan-seared sea bass with fava beans and peas risotto.

All six – The Musician *in extremis*

She moves through the fair – from weed, to mandrax, to crack. At the end of the jam she lies on the warehouse floor, foaming. Her guitar blitches and buzzes, like a dangerous animal – a rabid bat nobody wants to touch. To unplug the thing now would feel like casting her adrift forever.

41

THE TOWER

'The tower of the Graduate College was named the Ivory Tower, after the benefactor, whose company made Ivory Soap.'

Descartes teaches in this place of freedom, tranquillity and leisure. A storm might topple a young king and queen from even their most modest aspirations. Their crowns would fall off, and a fool might catch one and feel ennobled. He writes to a priest that even in barbarous societies no one is allowed to teach known untruths. A few stars fall in sympathy, softly.

1st – The Tower of Presumption
Foundations already resemble a ruin, an encampment of the salvage gang, or one of the deniable *favelas*. Artists and locals grumble about the giant finger, an insult to our age. This new egolith outsoars the underclass – the practice set, the race of clay – slighted in that distant tower of their own.

2nd – The Bell Tower
A captive view was never so panoramic. How thrilling to gaze on blue hills and, down below, a rescuer darting stealthily from bush to bush. The gaoler is sleeping off his meal. Though trip wires abound and the bell is deafening, she is hopeful, threading gold into a tapestry, her future.

3rd – The Tower of Yearning

Its launch pad is the shimmering cloud of its rising, the philosopher's baited breath. One storey at a time takes pleasure further, dismissing preposterous objections. Through discharge to bliss, the psyche seeks the lowest level of tension: the plain you can see more of by climbing.

4th – The Fish Tower

Pilchards are a pretext for a party. First they are sighted and hallooed from the low cliff, not quite safe without a tower. Deep waters broil: you might imagine a whale here. Down on the beach the watchman walks among dozens decanting his multitude. Invisible shepherd of souls.

5th – The Border Tower

There is no more heartening hearth than a fire well in a giant's vernacular barbican. The river is sleepy. Books in the library look undersized. Some tell tonight of the fi-fo-fum of dawn cattle raids against valley farmsteads. Straw is our bed and hooch our bedtime drink. Lust is our bedtime story.

6th – The Ornamental Tower

The hermit and the wallaby are happy enough merely to be glimpsed; the raven expects more attention. This fragment of portcullis, smothered in ivy, was smuggled from Chinon. You walk there and back before lunch. On your return to the big house, the alliances have shifted markedly.

All six – The Twin Towers

This meltdown irradiates the world. Fear and rage displace the elements. Who are we now? The escapees: the executive insisting on his refund; the tourist who witnessed a raid on a jeweller's; the secretary whose mother had an urgent need of her company, scattering ashes in Strawberry Fields.

42

THE MAZE

'When the Field Marshal pulled down all the city's minarets to confuse the occupying army, memory was promoted to the level of valour.'

Which came first, maze or sheepfold? Unarmed, listening intently, head full of shadowy myths, you step undaunted into destiny. Turning a corner you almost bump into a man who resembles your father, with shears in his hand. Is there blood on the blades? Later you notice how flat the cliffs of green are, how bright the cuts on leftover leafy sprigs at your feet.

1st — The Maze in the Temple Tiles
Curtains ripple in the breeze, soldiers watch with folded arms. Why not walk straight to the bull's-eye, insist on your due? Because whisperers dislike straight lines, that's what shouts are for, from stone to stone across a lake: there has to be time for you to be ashamed of your imperfections.

2nd — The One-way Maze
The hand is removed from the hedge when the sum of your turns reaches zero — with a compass you can find the exit. Imagine the inside of a G, touring anticlockwise, veering rightwards at the top of the downstroke. In reverse the algorithm fails, and you're lost if the heart feels like home.

3rd – The Treacherous Maze

The paradigm is the brain's convolutions, weighing attainment of the seed pearl against relief at getting out unmolested. The first challenge for those with a plan is a simple question: is this line a wall or a pathway? A fatal fog confuses every turn. Somewhere brutish nostrils are twitching.

4th – The Maize Maze

Choose your artificer wisely: a lost farm boy may be tempted to carve illicit arches with his cutter. Delayed cutting keeps the foliage greener longer, reducing the fire risk. Hallowe'en night shows, however, are ill advised: customers are likely to unshroud any threat with their lighters.

5th – The Imperial Maze

Copper radiance, blazing omnipotence – full baroque revelation. Cascades of spray are like a time-lapse with galloping weather. Hearing the fountain from an adjacent alley, humbly you withdraw and return: the protocol. Destination sun: nowhere to go but outwards, back into the shadows.

6th – The Most Serene Maze

The address system rivals Tokyo's. Where else can you see the despair of visitors who are *not* lost? They struggle to escape the ubiquitous *Per San Marco* signs. Somewhere there must be a chink in a wall! Beyond the sector of second homes: the periphery, where the purest dialect is spoken.

All six – The Moral Maze

Yuck! This is the place to turn back, the final retching post. Call your dog to heel and wipe off its slobber. Never mind what promises you made to thugs and thieves: return to the straight and narrow. The path runs along the *tops* of tall hedges! On either side are terrifying bottomless chasms.

43

HAIR

'A bad hair day is a day that only starts with uncontrollable hair. The truth is, the mirror gods will often relent by lunchtime.'

Who would have guessed the Cleopatra fringe would be so short-lived? Many suspect foul play: an actress, it's thought, bought by a rival studio, may have slipped an asp into the Hollywood harem. Revivals turn heads. But this is no forgiving cut: sharp angles sit ill with strong cheekbones, nose or jaw. The ideal face for such a frame is oval, round or heart-shaped.

1st – The Hair in Its Proper Place

That spin pin does the job of twenty kirby pins without snagging or faltering. In the hands of a maestro you're marble with the attributes of never-mentioned flesh – pliable as wax, cleaving to the skilful hand. The frisson between stylist and styled gives all good hair its élan.

2nd – The Hair Bulletin

There's bubbly in the newsrooms for a syndicated scoop – a smirk-and-tell spectacular. Driving a golfball into the rough of a celebrity photo mag; grey-sheeted at the Maltese barber's: the first bearded TV newsreader. Surprisingly, he speaks from the voice box, in a timbre slightly feminine.

3rd – The Hair Reflected

The *deuxième toilette*, for a gentleman caller who loves her in a six-way mirror: hexagonal joy, met with politeness. Exquisite downcombing parts tangled filaments of the golden waterfall. Disdained by servants, he's back now in the cold grey street, a priceless treasure bundled in his heart.

4th – Hairless in Gaza

Most days a reassuring morning mist blankets the furrows, soft-focus idyll of fieldwork – rough-and-ready life skills. Today, intimacy is the paradox of a scripted surprise on which the ploughshare thuds, as the all-knowing priestess lays herself out for adoration, amidst a clattering of jackdaws.

5th – The Bad Hair Day

Tented from the chin down, he smiles in the mirror at his executioner. Neapolitan scissors, with twirls like moustaches, groom him for an interview. Then a crisis, worse than an earthquake at the dentist's. A conflagration in one ear! Protestations. The other tuft pointlessly saved.

6th – The Hair Trade

Prison and temple supply the global need – wardens shear captives like sheep, while acolytes give freely, in gratitude for answered prayers. In the desert town where two rivers almost meet, extension agents scout and trade. Camels are laden, plying the keratin road through a veil of sand.

All six – The Hair in a Polish Plait

Cut it off and the malady will take its revenge: even kings have been enslaved to this appendage of filthy knots which courtiers might copy to show solidarity. What are the nightmare symptoms, other than the plait itself? Rheumatic aches; cravings, sometimes for costly imported wine.

44

THE SPY

'Scalp hunters, babysitters, ferrets, pavement artists walk at least once around the block before entering any building.'

Some agents use national security surveillance to track their lovers – past, present, would-be, fantasy – in the manner of a policeman 'running a plate for a date'. They might just be practising; or testing new paradigms. Often a blind eye is turned, since operatives who feel shame under close observation waste time and energy trying to outwit the controllers.

1st – The Spy at Court
Onion and lemon juice are so often used as invisible inks that any blank paper is suspect. The playwright's stationery is impounded, turning him against the state. His scripts are tested for acrostics. When the queen threw her slipper at him, years ago, was this a coded execution warrant?

2nd – The Downtown Spy
The address is an abortion clinic. Alpha (1 hour, followed by 4 hours) has had a consultation, then an abortion. Bravo (8 hours, week days) works there. Charlie (10 hours, most week days) is a protester. Delta (half an hour, weekly) is a trans person who visits regularly for hormones.

3rd – The Christmas Spy

Top of the gift list is a Ninja mitten sock, for climbing trees and scaling walls. Second is a book with encrypted diagrams on spycraft, including taking patience to the nth degree. The calendar's trapdoor often shows boring school. The time will come to stake out the hearth in a soot suit.

4th – The Industrial Spies

Silk fills the war chest by the law of attraction. Without tearing it will penetrate a wound with the arrowhead, facilitating extraction. The world is rebalanced by two monks, watering mulberries even as their thirst rages, smuggling silkworm larvae in hollow walking sticks to Byzantium.

5th – The Domestic Spy

With trust in the world dissolved, a locked door is an all too obvious clue; ditto the libidinous vibrating mobile. A traditionalist's sudden interest in new kinds of music may prove alarming. All lovers start out as detectives. But knowledge may be too dangerous a template for modern loving.

6th – The Spy Centre

Brainwashing is as easy as car washing – HQ has a neuroscience wing. A mini-skirted robot leads visitors through their own labyrinth, insulated from the staff labyrinth. The chief's lair is an underground bunker a mile from the periphery. School parties are bemused by the *faux* radial layout.

All six – The Psychic Spy

An astrophysicist tests the agency's remote viewer, setting questions in sealed envelopes. A non-scientist, he describes an electron right down to its spin states. He sketches a waveform. Yet his predictions are flawed: a teenage right-to-work law; a world superstate governed by technocrats.

45

THE RIVER

'The mellifluous name is peculiar to English: locals splutter on a tangle of consonants — a cormorant's nest, with ramparts of broken vodka bottles.'

Lingering here is unsettling, holding you back from your longings. From the fissure in mountain roughness most people gravitate downstream, knee-deep in alpine flowers, feeling the delta's pull – the great escape, the lure of houseboats with their clever little cupboards, wine bottles cooling in a rope sling, glassy bootlace elvers endlessly weaving nothing.

1st — The Youthful River
Enthusiasm gurgles, chubby splayed fingers of innocence waving in a brave new element: air. The life force is welcome here: even heather makes all the mistakes of youth. When the exhausted salmon shows up, it spawns as if to prove the point, unable to rest in this turbulent nursery.

2nd — The Festive River
Drinking booths, arbours, mazes and alleys raise high a carnival from the frozen river iced enough for salted braziers burning purple and green. In his drunkenness a courtier upsets a fire basket, but no harm is done. Scrape the frost and you'll see the flounder halted in its gentle wave.

3rd – The River Bank Refectory

A brood forms a circular queue in a sand burrow. There's an azure flash with its catchlight of silver – a minnow presented, minute in the formal moment, to the chick in the opening. A little gulp, then off the fishwife flies. They shuffle round, tick-tock of gapes, most urgent tiny hungers.

4th – The Conflicted River

Sturgeon have returned to the *cloaca maxima*: this rumour hangs in the fog like a memory of mint on the steppes. Then one day a big fish is landed. The heart lifts, then sinks again – it's a scrofulous eyesore dragged onto a beach of clay pipe shards upstream of the Romany bathing bank.

5th – The Royal River

The unique celebratory proposition is oars and hulls at random angles – the 'Canaletto moment'. At the knot of the plume, a Venetian barque, with a medley of grim and smiling faces, the jubilee of quick-slow dynastic succession. The Thames is getting wilder, the sewers straining.

6th – The Indomitable River

When a head of state swims naked in a river, these days he keeps his clothes in a locker – not piled on the bank where a lady journalist might sit on them, demanding an interview. Even ice will seldom obstruct history: water slithers on its belly, a commando beneath the searchlights.

All six – The Valedictory River

How well the most watchable action fits a picture of stillness, distance, reflectiveness – the view towards the ocean. High on the bluff the elders settle into their estate, the relaxing vista of offspring tracing curves along the mudflats. Farther out, hazy red sails are native, scarcely moving.

46

THE MOON

'The bone-dry moon that churns a planet's seas is the ghostly pale moon dislodging a gender's blood.'

The myth of snow-white Raven stealing sun, moon, stars and water from the eaves of Grey Eagle's longhouse is for first-year creative writing. Try practical science instead: the elements corresponding with roots, seeds, leaves, flowers; plus lunar astrology. With the waxing of the moon the earth exhales. Waxing is for seeding, fruiting; waning for maintenance.

1st – The Intimate Moon
A full moon after a super full moon is bigger and brighter than an average full moon – and may be overpraised, a month too late. A super full moon in the northern winter looks larger than its summer equivalent: the sun, reaching around our planet from behind, hugs the satellite closer to itself.

2nd – Spaceship Moon
The 'whack' theory is absurd: a second collision to adjust the angular momentum would have been *so* unlikely! Many of the ratios are base-ten integers. Discarded modules make the moon ring like a bell. Its message, in metrics and megalithic yards: 'Go back in time; hang me like a medal.'

3rd – The Moonlight Sonata

Like raindrops, grace notes free-fall into the piano factories of the Ruhr – fortissimo! Conservatory-trained camp kommandants were thought to be pitch perfect. Beethoven huddled in his shelter, his hearing already kaput. Choirs of allied angels take inspiration from a dog-eared atlas of craters.

4th – The Wet and Dry Moons

Some skywatchers speak of the upturned crescent as the wet moon, a bowl brimming with winter rain and snow. Hawaiians, too roseate for drowning, have their Dripping Wet Moon month. For others the imagined full bowl is dryness briefly relished: it has yet to tilt to pour out its summer floods.

5th – The Ominous Moon

The asylum porch light is on the blink, confused by clouds. When the moon sits full, its edge cuts sharp and can't be wholly sheathed. A clan of *Urvolk* wreaks demented havoc. Some enlightened surgeons warn that victims who make it to hospital face the problem of less effective clotting.

6th – The Man on the Moon

Your second-hand Ford has a computer a thousand times cleverer. A flag was planted (since there was none to capture), its ripples suggesting a breeze. No monkey scouted the silver canyons. But the real conspiracy was the lowballing of risk by mission control, the gamble on heroism.

All six – The Dealer's Moon

Crust, mantle and core form the quiet concentric chord that orchestrates the transfer of a small white packet on a dark bushy avenue of lighted windows, the old embankment. The moon has secrets it will keep forever behind its confident alibi: a pearl, weeping, in the goblet of milky sky.

47

THE ACTOR

'Calling the director a vampire, in rehearsals, won for her the love of all the cast, except his mistress, playing Snow White.'

Inhabiting a tree is formative. From fingers browning and falling you progress to almost visible roots, then later to cruelly self-examining in the round, the *bourgeoisie* undressed, shielded by a dustbin lid. A bonfire of fancy dress brings authentic renewal. It's feeding time in the theatre: the actor eats off bare boards the delirium from which he was born.

1st – The Student Actor

Ambition travels radially along the bus routes, like a brushfire. To have a skull on your mantelpiece, where an Oscar would sit less broodily! This is a play so vast, it's a system – an ambient electricity. Oh, to be a dark lean planet in the existential north, drinking the energy of southern souls!

2nd – The Actor Reciting Poetry

The words are imperious: syntax wraps itself around them, like a consul's cloak tossed in patrician gestures. What we lose is the flowering heart; what we learn is that language is a notation of itself. 'Please trust me with my own performance,' says the steam to the kettle, misting the windows.

3rd – The Actor of the Floating World

Find the pillow diarist among ticket touts, squid sellers, truant servants. The shrine maiden will read to you about bringing her dry riverbed shows to the court; then the ban on women, then boys, then double suicides, on stage. Admire the styles of the face, morphing towards peak drama.

4th – The Actor in Flight from the Self

Escape velocity is attained twice: first, the allure of a hiding place to speak from; then the young giant you pretended to be, spotless skin, filling the screen with the wrong squeeze. It's you, evidently, kissing. Old films disappoint: the girl you long to see again is always off camera.

5th – The Method Actor

You put on a stovepipe hat and build a cabin, and the right way to speak just comes to you. Then you hold that voice through the coffee breaks, while lesser actors keep their everyday thoughts to themselves. If you didn't shoot it, don't eat it; and don't shout 'Shoot!' unless you mean it.

6th – The Actress and the Bishop

Under the sheets: he and his favourite leading lady, surrounded by a crew of sparks. She's always on time, knows her lines and does her own hair and make-up. *Double entendres* work best out of context, but nonetheless are scripted for bedroom scenes. It works because nothing ever happens.

All six – The Actor's Nemesis

Timely prompting died with Wolfitt. In any case, the storm machine is turned up to max, the stage manager cranking away, unable to reach the prompt book, which is soaked – the stage has no convincing substitute for water. He dries while naked, on the heath with a word-perfect fool.

48

THE ROSE

'A yellow rose means:"Don't you love me any more?"A rose with blackfly means: "I wash my hands of you!"'

Flower losses are easily dealt with. Pull the affected petals off or snip the whole head. Ignore the complacent camellia, smiling unarmed at its enemies. War can shake up any court, dress uniforms slashed in battle. Ordinary armies feel the stress first, ending up in tatters, too exhausted for mourning; then the state as a body suffers, waking to a withered dawn.

1st – The Medieval Rose
Deer fell by the dozen, spreading *bonhomie*. The emperor ordered a mass in the forest and left the reliquary hanging on a wild rose. The Virgin's deer-slaying hair must be found! It was, but the object was inextricable from the tree, alive today, clinging to the apse of the hunter's cathedral.

2nd – The Hazardous Rose
Caged within a pergola, 'Kiftgate' is choleric and dangerous. Or if it captures an oak, branches brought down by autumn storms are panthers, suddenly your problem on a fateful morning – scars both physical and mental. One opts instead for the lax demeanour of 'Rambling Rector'.

3rd – The Old-fashioned Rose

The old roses are run to earth in sidelong places – tennis courts, almshouse yards, patches of land between butcher's and bakery. Too wise and decent to conspire, they make no attempt to reassert ascendancy: the enthusiasts – vicars, teachers, factory-owners's wives – will see to that on their behalf.

4th – The Rose Tattoo

The floriferous needle has brought the boldest template shinily to life, an allotment of cabbage roses spreading from buttocks to thigh and lower back, counterpoint to the lithe body's torque. Those who once lusted for her naked rear now see inky end-of-pier damask chasteningly draping it.

5th – The Rose Garden

Campaign dreams are often of special places. She wakes from a nap in the Oval Office – the President is busy in the press room. Tempted by a glowing afternoon, she strolls into the Rose Garden. Fragrant 'Monica Lewinksy' has vanished. Orange 'Laura Bush' flares like a Texas sunset.

6th – The Self-healing Rose

Sports concealed in the inner layer of the meristem can break free if you take a root cutting, wreaking fancy havoc with the establishment – a petal defiantly striped, a rebel's battle flag; or a raggedy two-tone leaf. Yet the nation is resilient – designed to starve its outlaws, soon forgotten.

All six – The Mystic Rose

Chevalier of the pelican! Working late at the museum, he sees the rose hover and vibrate again, infinitely expanded goddess of the night withering on the atomic cross, shedding petals on parquet. Most others would be uncomfortable here. He sweeps discarded raiments into his pan.

49

THE ELEPHANT

'May you feel the loving presence of Ganesh on his birthday (1st September) and on yours. Namaste.'

Using trunks to test unsafe ground, these Atlas elephants were surer than mountain goats. They widened the passes for the army – contrary to popular belief. Their problem was lack of browse. Napoleon may have found a few bones, kept them as mementoes. Where he came across Hannibal's name on alpine rocks he carved his own name underneath.

1st – The War Elephant
Tough leggings disable hamstring attacks, while armour on the leather cinch stops enemies from hacking at the hoodah strap and bringing down the tower where the mahout sits behind the fan-shaped helmet shield. Out front, between sword-fitted tusks, the trunk flails its chain mace.

2nd – The Elephant Riders
Three mahouts meet at the temple. One uses ingenuity, one pain, one love to control his elephant. Love's ingenuity is modest – after bathing, a massage with rocks and coconut husks. Poles and hooks in tender parts – let us not speak of this. Love's pain, even accidental, is never atoned for.

3rd – The Elephant as Propaganda

Alternating current is dangerous, but Westinghouse controls the electric
infrastructure. An elephant proves Edison's point. Having killed a keeper
who'd fed it a lit cigar, wired into copper sandals, silently it dies on film –
while calls below our hearing travel from Coney Island back to Borneo.

4th – The Utility Elephant

The hydrants of the Eastern metropolis are an elephant's blessing in a
heatwave, recycling rivers of rain in the underworld, relaying it to the
goddess who opens up clouds for her subjects' sakes, smiling irresistibly
through her soaking, at everyone responsible enough to wield a spray cap.

5th – The Circus Elephant

Foam on the stable floor at mucking out should have been a warning.
Black temporin runs into the mouth, there's a swelling behind the eyes,
the hind legs are wet with urine. A Swiss town shakes apart. Fusiliers are
called; then tanners and taxidermists, laid off when civic funding failed.

6th – The Elephant in the City

In memory of Jules Verne, it stomps down Threadneedle Street – all
pistons and motors, with twenty-two *manipulateurs* visible like the organs
in a shrimp. Each time a giant foot lands, it sends out a puff of dust. Soon
they'll destroy the beast: it's sickening from a surfeit of invitations.

All six – The Elephant Tribute

Just as the trunk has many uses, such as trumpeting alarm or raising itself,
arm-like, in greeting, so does the tusk, as seen in battles on a baize veldt,
masterpieces for hands and ears, and self-depiction – observe Justinian's
Phrygian subjects, one leading an elephant, one with bejewelled ivory.

50

THE FATHER

'Unconscious fathers, a diaspora of wanderers at large on the sea of souls, share a bond known only to the pantheon's patriarch.'

Those who have never witnessed birth are an antique tribe with a second chance if the daughter is willing, as she might be if she truly understands. Generations fold into themselves, an asymmetric wave, endlessly returning – yet farther each time from where you stand on the shore with your trident and net, and no spare hand to hold another's hand.

1st – The Enterprising Father
Equities fluctuate but his brow never crumples. High windows look away, playground grazes toughen. A tangled nerve ball bounces into adulthood. He is elsewhere, scourge of pirates, tirelessly working the sea lanes – returning home without any stories. His love is a virtuous calculus.

2nd – The Father of the Great Outdoors
The yellow ribbon of woodsmanship is for escaping camping, a skill extrapolated from guiles taught by fathers. Unwittingly they turn into predators, tamed by excuses, one of which strikes home. The campfire is short of a son, out there like a wolf, ruthless as the saga's heroes.

3rd – The Seasonal Father

The penultimate torture is the mirror in the lift between two floors – the man-eating beard. Surrogate sons and daughters are the angel's scorpion army. The grotto gives up its wounded. Later, the Iscariot family reunion: a speech is clamoured for, with rhythmic thumping on a big trestle table.

4th – The Father of the Tribes

Canada was a safe, sane house for a heliotropic family. An Ontario department store floorwalker was told one day of his royal native lineage: his father was grand vizier of a headhunter rainforest principality, playing the imperial system. Imagine finding a shrivelled head in your freezer!

5th – The Proud Father

Hercules threw javelins at targets from horseback, as well as for distance at the end of a run. This Zeus's habitat is a garden of beer and bindweed. On the brightest days the telly goes back indoors. He turns it on an hour before time: athletes have been crawling in traffic to get to the stadium.

6th – The Single Father

He makes up the quarrel with his sister and takes a market job, flexible for childcare. A booklet, *How to be a hands-on, heart-on father,* tells him: 'Dad sets the bar for future dates.' He feeds her, burps her; swings her. While she plays in a sandpit, he battles the *FT* on a windswept bench.

All six – The Incomparable Father

The four-bird roast is marvellous, its value imparting flavour. People drop by, unannounced! He collects sugar from cafés, pens from banks, yet his generosity flows like northern floodwater, swamping embarrassments. Even with heartbreak a wall away, you are always grateful beyond words.

51

THE HOSPITAL

'They know how people feel about their bodies. They know what things are used just once, then simply thrown away.'

If one or two fields are hollowed out for healing, surrounding plough-lands look anaemic, uninvolved. Surgeons and farmers rarely meet – though a tractor may slither down a mudbank. Brilliance is called for when the levee breaks. Relatives, as well as panickers among the public, will hamper evacuation; patients must be handcuffed to their records.

1st – The Field Hospital
The body has its own front line – urgent, ragged and noisy. The rattle of a bullet in a tin dish is just the beginning. Prisoners are afraid they might be used for experiments. When the morphine runs out, placebo M&Ms are distributed – each colour represents a different level of pain relief.

2nd – The Hospital Vestibule
The by-laws are lost, but someone's on the case – an orderly perhaps, or a Friend of Wellness. Meanwhile, a codger asserts his buttonholing rights, mumbling into his Levantine beard a parable of celestial triage, drowned in a concourse of echoes. He has some problem also with his palette.

3rd – The Hospital Lunch

The conjurer lifts the lid on a sad surprise: vegetables huddled together anxiously, as if on their first night at the zoo. There's no rota for changing the rota, so once again the cold end of the ward savours the tasteless hors d'oeuvres of expectation. The trolley stalls. Lunch is a two-hour interlude.

4th – The Enlightened Hospital

There's a living wall; there's a Zen garden in a light-well. The nit lady finds an acupuncture needle in a girl's hair. A nurse, washing her hands, focuses without judgement on warm water, soap, and where she is in the clinical environment – at the basin, a mild chronic pain behind her brow.

5th – The Hospital City

It's a mile back to the ward: your symptoms may complicate. Nurses often use scooters, surgeons skateboards. Sometimes there's a known Dr Hodad ('hands of death and destruction'), perhaps a drinker, or someone who likes to offer virtuosity, a special service, VIPs being most at risk.

6th – The Exclusive Hospital

So you covet the room with three sofas and a balcony with a perfect view of the wicket? Make your bid by all means: many fear such attentions, the final luxury, so the room might well be free. As you sit at the window knitting, relish the shattering of stumps, the healing power of willow.

All six – The Working Hospital

The holy of holies is the grail long imagined, though one is seldom if ever in the moment. It's all handing over and thanklessly taking, peering and fiddling, and mumbling into masks. The communicants speak staccato in various accents. Stay with us. You are the wafer and the wine.

52

THE BREAKFAST

"'Wink at your grocer and see what you get!"— the sweetheart of the toasted corn, smiling from a cereal packet, wholesome, hugging a golden sheaf.

The dream is a jar of honey, smashed on terracotta tiles: you knew it would slip through your fingers. Having enjoyed another sweet night unguarded, you understand the risks you took, sharp shards of reality. All you can do is drop the biggest chunks in the waste and sweep up the splinters; then start again with breakfast – amnesiac kippers or porridge.

1st – The Wild Breakfast
The first thing, after putting up the tents and digging the latrine, is to scout for a reliable safe, for your spring water and cloudberries. Map it in an all-weather notebook. Individual ziplocks of muesli prompt murmurs, the formula a mystery. A rock can be a little private room: do not disturb.

2nd – Breakfast in Bed
The tray is an encumbrance. Surfaces are not just up and down: they crumple, invading the middle space between horizontal planes. Throw the book of etiquette out of the window – except that the window can't be opened! You might as well be swimming in reeds or cycling in soft sand.

3rd – The Honeymoon Breakfast

The best man's speech referred with due permission to her bump. Elderly aunts exchanged knowing looks. Now officially she's breakfasting on nutrients, unexpectedly in the dining room, savouring her long afternoon of love and happiness, proud of her crescent glow, her morning moon.

4th – The Breakfast on the Early Morning Train

A lightly poached egg scarcely wobbles on the plate, though a metronome warns of mortality. The romantic lilt of the adventurous express! Imagine Mongolia all around, eagle trainers waking; or Russia with its Cossacks, mounted on the wind, suddenly noticed alongside the dining carriage.

5th – The Breakfast Meeting

Through a plate-glass panorama of skyscrapers a low sun shines on the same old, same old neologisms. It's turnover time, takeover time for competitive souls. American karma, the sweetest kind, ripples through the long day ahead. What's it to be? Egg on a tie or ink on a letter of intent?

6th – The Alpine Breakfast

Mountains thrive on valley harvests – not just cows on the green shoulders of white-haired giants. A little narrow-gauge egg train chugs up from the chicken lands, dirt yards canton frontiers cross. Grains too are brought, and fish, and foster children, hampered by lowland schools.

All six – The Breakfast on the Field of Gold

An ordinand, in a refulgent gown, serves orange juice, one hand behind her back like a wine waiter. There's a choice of newspapers: broadsheet, tabloid, all of them white on white. A majestic rooster rends the silence. Miles off, the chuck of an axe at the dark edge of the forest of fugitives.

53

THE MAP

'Time traveller seeks part-time assistant with traditional humanist values: must be good around old maps. Non-smoker. Sense of humour.'

Contours are ignored until they squeeze together. Brown is tough and closest to the sky; green may flood at any time; blue is the idleness of perfection. Instead of a church, an ecumenical shield brandished by a p.o.w. No deer or rabbits: just the occasional duck, hawk or puffin. Old tracks persist, since certain ghosts will never forsake their horses.

1st – The Map of Faith
Two bare feet – islands with southern inlets – signal perambulatory powers, the pilgrim's readiness. The navel is the holy city, the umbilical river near by. The head is the thule of paradise, walled off, first couple and serpent in a memory palisade. Angels and demons watch from the corners.

2nd – The Map of Knowledge
At the thoughtful centre of chaos the cartographer engraves a web of history – the spider of civilisations growing fat on risk. Legend is the mirror of lost witness. Jason plies his day job, importing dragon skulls to Alexandria. The island of California is unbirthed back to its mother.

3rd – The Map of the Reconstruction

The 'sworn viewer' finesses a royal licence to map the new city after the fire. Vignettes of loss escape the court censor – a destroyed paint factory exposed to the diluting sky, a blackened prison fatal to loving visitors as well as inmates. Griefs underfoot are bright modern hope's foundation.

4th – The Tattooed Map

The forensic team turns up at the parlour of tawdry tattoos, cartographic ashes warm in the grate. But the treasure's location ripples on an inside thigh, the client miles away, lost in the badlands of desire, sweet betrayals by seductresses the Black Hand gang will surely brief in the erotic arts.

5th – The Map Sale

A crozier marks the spot. The nave and chancel belong to the four winds: a gamble on futures has dropped off the edge of the ocean. Zoom in on the treasury. Negotiations are afoot with a major auction house. The archivist has sent for a stronger travel box, with judder-proof hinges.

6th – The Parallax Map of the Lakes

For walkers who enjoy novelty, a graphic inspired by the famed masterpiece of the Underworld. Only up and down, and sideways, and both diagonals. Annotation lines up barn against spire, sheepfold against waterfall. No trace of Wainwright's ashes in their heathery home.

All six – The Mental Map

Such inner threads, of limited use to lost souls, may have dissolved anyway, a secret flaw like a deviated septum; or never have grown in the first place. A compass, useless in space, outperforms a map in the city's most intimate convolutions. The body's left and right assert their primacy.

54

THE DOG

'Little flags of the type more usually seen on sandcastles have been left atop piles of poo, bearing humorous yet caustic aphorisms.'

The heath is yours when upturned eyes implore. Outside it's suddenly your element. Grimly a weekday professional clutches his five-string bouquet of hybrid athletes, as if vacuuming the land. Off the leash there are hazards. You slink under a bush to lick your wounds, unwilling to face the world till you're whole again. Then you're called before you're ready.

1st – The Rain Dog
Our German forefathers, clipping close for swimming, left certain organs and joints their insulation muffs. A continental clip has shaven hind-quarters; an English saddle clip has three pom poms down each flank and hind leg. Rain dogs love to play in a sprinkler, on the lawns of the free.

2nd – The Dog Absolved from Blame
Hound of the dynasty of darkness: its two glowing eyes are fog lights of bloodthirsty ambition for a fashionable West End address. A phosphorus bath – indeed, the whole Gothic delusion – is the pathology of the metropolitan enlightenment. 'Elemental, my dear Watson, elemental!'

3rd – The Agile Dog

She clears an ascending triple-bar spread jump, then shows perfection
at the weave poles, the closed and open tunnels, the pause table, the
see-saw, the hanging tyre. But her handler used an umbrella on the walk-
through! The challenge is dismissed: all points awarded are allowed to stand.

4th – The Half Lap Dog

She calls him Fortinbras, her 'half lap dog'. A Great Dane's half-
hundredweight rear end on the tartan shelf of a pair of human thighs,
forelegs like tree trunks on the brewhouse café cobbles. Byron's début
Christmas dinner at Newstead would have been a fleeting snack to him.

5th – The Dog in Space

Catch a Moscow street mutt, used to extremes of cold and hunger
– a female (easier to manage the waste). Train her by progressively
reducing the cage size. Before the launch, bring her home to a hero's fuss
from your family, heart-warming prelude to the cold confines of space.

6th – The Attack Dog

Ennobling the sequoia avenue, a limestone monument of wolves tearing a
hind apart, savaged by time. A perpetrator hurtles towards you – slavering
asteroid, released from the vanishing point. The owner's reassurances of
play are as comforting as an offer of cocoa seconds before the blade falls.

All six – The Rescue Dog

It's quicksand's turn again but nobody has remembered the rope. They
weigh the options. Our heroine adopting a raccoon? Helping a farmer fill
in his tax return? In the end they plump for the fallen satellite. However,
the footage is mothballed – radiation has become an all-American phobia.

55

THE LIE

'Truth flutters on the mountain in the winds of change: all that matters is the pole, and the flag where it's tight at the pole.'

To secure the one remaining slice of pie you say there's a grub in it; then the inconvenient irony wriggles its little white finger, rejoicing in your double bind. All this is child's play. Ruthless anti-social climbers, tracking deceptions one by one in chains of ever more improbable logic, look back nostalgically to days of innocent thieving in the orchard of values.

1st – The Cretan Lie
In the mountains there's a tax on affluence – in the labyrinth of dirt tracks strewn with rocks, an uninsurable massacre of alimentary undersides by – frankly – a fat-arse jellyfish. Presented with the bill, he remembers those knocks and lurches. Sacrifice to the Minotaur silences the call to combat.

2nd – The Lie of Abbreviated Truth
Some send a *doppelgänger* to the valley church while talking to God on the mountain. Others rely on mental reservation: 'I have never studied abroad and that's the truth,' they say, adding inwardly: '...*for the purpose of self-preservation.*' Their fight against the barbarous heart lives on.

3rd – The Lie of the Third Reason

Only dullards aver that character is mountainous – it can drift like a delta
in the course of one long rambling sentence. 'Besides' is a prelude to the
coda of confession, the lie exhibited, disarming the sword of fate – like a
plagiarism foiled by involuntary clues dropped for all the world to see.

4th – The Punitive Lie

Then there's the lie within the carrier lie, the double poison: 'I told the
solicitor your maths isn't up to their homework.' In the punitive marriage
truth is withheld like cash, light or food – even a quick-start breakfast.
Defend your precious freedoms; sharpen your knife on the mountain.

5th – The Lie against Science

Drug mules who lose the stash end up at the mountain's foot – he'd
read this but failed to see the connection. The particle scientist's crime
was believing in a body the equal of his brain: a lingerie model, Russian.
Nobel laureates cite him still in their papers – the genius of tenure!

6th – The Lie Discovered

The estate is a maze with ears behind every hedge, and the watchful
peacock's scream penetrates as far as the Carlton Club. Don't assume
your dalliance with the mountain girl was fire-walled by box and beech:
there was a commoner within earshot, fussily re-roofing the duck house.

All six – The Lie Concealed

A mountain of a man in a corduroy suit, wobbling, sweating, eyes darting
every which way, even so he outwits the polygraph. A philosopher's
innocence, inhabited like armour, flatlines, dead to emotional pressures –
a *tour de force* of an acting style a million miles from the method.

56

THE VILLAGE

'The brave lives of the roundabout people, sharing the seasons and the stars, and keeping their smaller dramas to themselves.'

One village has farms down the main street! Another, a duck pond the size of Leicester Square. Advent is the yellow glow of windows in the year's midnight – curtains are paranoid. Twilight is the hour when salesmen wander abroad, peeking in – for example, the harmonium merchant, since music from a hill village carries far, its hymns already in the clouds.

1st – The Cave Village

Tourists are enticed to fervent flamencos at twilight – flame-haired señoritas in clouds of sandstone dust. A goat's-skull flagon is proffered as memento of the show, admission priced accordingly. On Mozarabic ramparts the Guardia check for torch flashes at half-hour intervals.

2nd – The Village of Prying Eyes

Telephonists listened in – remember them? Courtship was public, a connection between distant but familiar eccentricities. The postman knew the catalogue from the envelope, having checked the coded brand name online. You wanted to but daren't, and that too is in the public domain.

3rd – The Village of Sun and Shade

There are colonnades and *tempietti*. Memorabilia abound in the piazza –
as do the franchise police handing out copyright signs to photographers.
The captive stares accusingly, up through the leas of every teacup. Feed a
pound into the telescope: trace the estuary's tide climbing a heron's legs.

4th – The Swiss Village

This replica, built in Tennessee by a railroad magnate, was first a farm,
then a rehab centre. Now it stores embryos and semen to preserve the
genetic diversity of livestock. Meet the Poitou donkey, known for its
strength, named Peter; and the myotonic, 'fainting' goat named Heidi.

5th – The Hopeful Village

Their diet is fried rats, salads of unfashionable weeds, frogs from a lake
of sewage. A brothel owner who diversified found goats even more
troublesome. Horses painted like zebras were rented out for parties.
Today we toast the slum's first female graduate, in university champagne.

6th – The Drowned Village

Volts of anger: redundant wiring severed from its grid. There were fish
in the belfry, a scow cheating in a race fathoms above the old village play-
ground. Now summer drought force-feeds the drowned spire – useful for
divers, the archaeological beacon. The swallows' empire shrinks.

All six – The Plague Village

Do pathogens travel faster through woodland? That depends on the carrier,
the nature of meetings in clearings, and the wind's intentions. Here in
the bare uplands the villagers migrated from their own graveyard, though
living still within the bell's clangorous ambit, with frequent visits home.

57

THE TEACHER

'Instead of tassel and button, a mourning mortarboard is topped with a saltire of two black ribbons and, in the centre, a black ribbon rosette, grosgrain or satin.'

Having gathered up the grammars, he pushes the desks aside to clear a judo floor. First it's boy against boy, girl against girl; later he mixes genders. Grades are the business of the committed self, which needs, not a protective shell, but the skills of active development. The double life will fuse into one. The corporal reward for triers is a smiling tease or sarcasm.

1st – The Conqueror's Teacher

He points to a chariot: 'Behold a new-found creature. Refute.' For the boy's sake he edits and annotates the *Iliad*. Years later the conqueror finds the ideal repository for this most precious gift. From a gem-studded casket in the ransacked Persian court he tips healing unguents onto the tiled floor.

2nd – The Teacher at Large

The lanes are unsafe: a gang might hurtle around a sharp bend. Between capers they spy on Geography, as they call him. Mud-clad, like rugby players, they slither through wintry hedges. In Wellingtons he walks his Pomeranian, the sight and smell of pipe smoke guiding their pursuit.

3rd – The Modernist Teacher

He walks backwards into the classroom, spins around and flourishes two commas on the blackboard, one inverted. 'This is Columbus, swimming to the New World.' Then a fish; then a fisherman's line, all over the place. 'You are all sitting still, in a spiritual coma. Get weaving. Get drawing.'

4th – The Teacher of Nature

Birds dramatise a habitat – the field guide's art alive and industrious. A reed warbler, dashing to safety. Butterflies flitting, dragonflies hovering prior to darting. 'Prudent pond dippers, don't miss a food pass over your heads! Keep one eye on the sky. There's more to life than the syllabus!'

5th – The Teacher of Light

The teacher's subject is this: that he'll never make you stand in a corner. His suffering extinguishes your demerits. His kindness shines through brusque reports. Transformation within the curriculum! His miracles are those of the abstract artist proving he can draw if he wants to.

6th – Teachers under Siege

Gunfire, explosions. A teacher smears herself with blood, lies still in a flowerbed. In a crawl space above the casino, ten adults learn of their plight from their cell phones: grenades thrown like maize to chickens. Another teacher teaches the six non-Muslims to recite the Shahada.

All six – The Teacher of Souls

The school prayer's remit is brain and brawn, in equal measure. Everyone stands in assembly – in an hour there'll be fencing or exams in the same hall. The white-haired headmaster shows an OT charisma. He chalks up these initials. *Caret*: an extra T, added by some mild-mannered graffitist.

58

THE STAIRS

'Building codes usually treat alternating tread stairs as ladders: they are allowed only where ladders are allowed. You can't turn around on them.'

Ladders make for a treacherous descent. From a staircase you can aim a pistol or survey your admirers – and they you, head steady over a cascading dress, descending between hidden friezes, prompting a commotion on both sides of the oak wood, of falling nymphs and rising satyrs, hidden among leaves and acorns, Pan piping you to landfall.

1st – The Miracle Stairs

The Vatican's double helix was for mules, likely to get entangled together on meeting. In fact, there are two such staircases, though only the more recent is in use. The down ramp is an exit, the up ramp a papal enigma – emergency entrance for cavalry, or coachloads of invited symbologists.

2nd – The Staircase of Fire

Their men being absent, on some distant front, the unit is a regiment of women, offered fire bombs in exchange for husbands. Station bonds are unbreakable, as if held by a new glue that terrific heat only strengthens. The expanding staircase takes them to a midnight, fire-lit annealing.

3rd – The Stairs of No Resistance

A monk at Adam's Peak describes the method: you're not climbing, you're falling forwards, legs trailing behind a relaxed intention. 'Let your top half work for you,' he says ... at which point you stop and look at him askew, and he melts into the stone steps. The precipice towers above you.

4th – The Sunset Staircase

A new part in a neglected house gives grief nonetheless: the seat drive unit makes a banging noise mid-flight. A missing bracket has made the seat lean weirdly, deforming the joint in the middle of the rail. Knowing this doesn't really help: the question *What next?* can never be answered.

5th – The Baroque Staircase

The hall is like a marble church's nave, the volume of a hamlet of cottages – a perfect venue for the pantomime. A Solomonic pillar makes a brilliant beanstalk. The staircase is packed with children, the biggest up in the gods – a strange inversion of perspective to the architect playing Jack.

6th – The Staircase to Heaven

The naval antenna was a wire flung from peak to peak. The stair is for personnel only; hikers are banned. Scale the state asylum's fence and get to the trailhead by 3am if you plan to see the sunrise. Don't let climbers with machetes alarm you: the only other way is through dense bamboo.

All six – The Winding Stair

What makes a true and perfect lodge? Seven masters, five entered apprentices, a day's journey from a burroughs town without bark of dog or crow of cock. All odd numbers are men's advantage: the Vitruvian orders, the liberal sciences, the senses. The stair leads up to the doling of wages.

59

THE APPLE

'An apron sagging with apples, red and green: the well-beloved, the Eve of the fair, the promise.'

The apple draws the earth as much as the earth draws the apple. Grafts were taken from the gravity park where genius found sanctuary from lawlessness. One scion growing outside college gates gives a moment's foothold to a student dropping into his saucy night's adventure, seizing an apple as he drifts through the loving stair light of the lonely moon.

1st – The Apples of the West
The tor rises out of mist and marsh, the orchards hug high ground. Ley lines point back into the kingdom's heart, and outwards, westwards, to Avalon. Wake from long slumbers and breakfast on pippins – rosy ones. Gird yourself to battle against the sunset. Sink heroically into legend.

2nd – The Apple Undermined
Camouflaged, minuscule, the railroad worm feasts on the browning apple, a time ship starved for its short flight to earth, where the pupa overwinters. The fly mimics the foreparts of the four-eyed jumping spider. Innocent above such pitiful subterfuge, the apple tree rides the clouds.

3rd – The Apple and the Bullfinch

White rumps defiantly bob and dart in their market. To consume a bud, a plant chick, is to strangle hopeful industry at birth. The realism of survival is anti-pastoral: bale twine on one bough, fertiliser bags on another. Bravely they mate among the enemy – the true *sprezzatura*!

4th – The Apple Blossom Ultimatum

We trip on transgression, defying the settlement plan foisted on middle age. It's autumn, there's no time to spare. Can we sneak our way into ripeness, the fresh kind, with no trace of dissolution yet? One more blossom time might be given to us. Kick the tree: make it suck more sap.

5th – The Apples Afloat

Splashing about and getting soaked, the apple fleet refusing to quit its regatta on the waves, feels like a hopeless ritual invented a minute ago by children. In the cider fields, where a surplus is fair game for any ancient rigmarole, the real test for many is waiting to be plucked in marriage.

6th – The Emblematic Apple

The codebreaker's cyanide is absorbed into the mythic miasma: Snow White besmirched by persecution. Or is it that the bite conveys scale, a mouth for comparison? The anagram of postlapsarian colours has a logic instructive for the nursery. Green sits at the top, where the leaves are.

All six – The Five-pointed Apple

A matchmaker blacksmith of the Orne forges a blade of steel so fine he could present a father with two perfectly fitting hemispheres, each with its central pentagram: losel and damsel. This is the eloquence of steel and flesh: observe the exact placement of pips and follow their runic lust.

60

THE WORD

*'Words receiving the gift of happiness; words conferring the gift of happiness.
What a day of wonders!' (ancient Chinese picnic scroll)*

Some words are skins of wild beasts, others satin or gold. Some fly, some
crawl, shrivelling upon inspection; others stay majestically still. One will
clamber from the rubble of collapsed temples, safe in a world without
rescuers. Others can be wrung from us, like water from a rag; or stay
inside, festering. Yet even in the vaguest utterance there is perfect order.

1st – The Mythical Words
Stumbling in a drift of snow-with-bird prints, the abominable wordsmith
looms in a flurry of memes. Watch his blue lips, slicing counterparts
of tropic abundance in a land so thinly spread with phenomena. A hundred
words for drunkenness pour out of his mouth, a meltwater torrent.

2nd – The Safe Word
You'd be ill advised to opt for the password to your savings, a release into
penury. Better would be your birthplace or first pet, delivering you back
to the only innocence, the womb's, or padding towards you, potent spirit
animal, the keys to your cage jangling in slobbering jaws.

3rd – The Bygone Words
Archaism is a return to nature, digging wilted commonplaces back into the soil – and finding sovereigns at your feet. How refreshing in this alien realm where beardless blockheads in the emperor's new clothes render acronyms in lower-case letters – if one's pupils are to be believed!

4th – The Repeated Word
Today you learn to automate your mantra. Proceeds flow to hospitals, prisons, reservations. From any mantra you can tell the teacher's gender and graduation year. You imagine the seed word is Vedic, then discover it's Tantric! There should be a faintness, a melting like a cough drop.

5th – The Word Child
A smile for no reason, confusing in the absence of either joke or misery. It's private, like tears – bringing double danger to the honest apprentice lost in the mirrored ballroom of secret conventions. You wonder where you saw the advert: 'Emotional literary lessons. Half-price. Guaranteed.'

6th – The Words in the Whispering Gallery
Theatrical whispers in the round are challenging even when you live and breathe the language. Groundlings muffle the acoustics. You need to be first or last in the queue to the sacristy. Reporters licensed for blasphemy brandish the few choice words that will rise above the commotion.

All six – The Word and the Flesh
Host and hostel are not like flock and sky, more like two colours of smoke merging. Either may start to disappear long before the other. Word has the more obvious need, flesh the deeper. A person with hands touching, flesh on flesh, magics away the difference, subject and object transcended.

61

THE SHEPHERD

'If you make a hit movie about a shepherd's wife in Romania, the next role you're offered will be a pig farmer's wife in Spain.' (anonymous film actress)

His grandfather called things by their Norse names: 'mowdies' (moles), 'mel' (posthammer). He screams at his dog, swears at his son, curses rain, forms, hikers, pen pushers. In winter he pours over flock books. The Scar holds summer snow. Selling the perfect Herdwick (how white its ears were!), he misses it like a Rembrandt, gone from his living room wall.

1st – The Satanic Shepherd
A fiery voice inspired him, guarding his sheep while he lifted, with ease, the huge foundation stone. His coffin, tumbled downstream from the derelict brothel on the broken bridge, was beached and opened, eighty years after interment. Inside was a wolf's skeleton, skull grinning.

2nd – The Shepherd's Son
Late lambing can take place in the pasture. The boy learns to gambol and to flint a fire. His father may be Theocritus in fancy dress. A lamb with a black patch on one leg, athletic shadow self, will one day carry his flag of faith and victory at the games, to the gods' deafening uproar of acclaim.

3rd – The Shepherd as Hamlet

Sheep skulls are empirical, though their fine zigzag cracks are the ultimate delicacy, unimaginable, and cranial sump holes yearn for vessels like fields for stone walls. In fern drifts a skull might be stumbled upon by a ghost-blasted, raven-harried agriculture student far beyond the battlements.

4th – The Emigrant Shepherd

Perfect ease is out of the question, as in *any* country. But you get the land for nothing. The sheep, in a genial climate, are touched by neither fly nor foot-rot. Vile bushrangers can be softened with a bribe. Any ne'er-do-well should make a decent fist of being a shepherd in Van Diemen's Land.

5th – The Shepherd on the Eve of Insurrection

He sits on a crag in his broad-brimmed hat, lifting his eyes to the golden city, then back to his book, on loan under the scheme that's teaching him literacy. It seems to be a call to arms, though it's hard to be sure. If so, this book will be his weapon, not those rope-handled shearing blades.

6th – The Work Experience Shepherd

Now he knows what the crook is for: catching by the neck the ewes that need help with birthing. His job is pin them to the barn floor while the expert, this time, pushes the head back up the birth canal, first looping a cord around the one foot sticking out: normally it's both, of course.

All six – The Available Shepherd

The Internet drives tradition into its fold. Shepherding never sounded so alluring, nor so precarious, as in this 360-degree tour of an examined life. The water that runs through his hands is for sharing; the sheep that run over these hills are for shearing. In summer he's a paddle steamer pilot.

62

THE MOUSE

'Exchange of habits is a high-risk adventure. The town mouse drowns in butter, the country mouse drowns in gin.'

Scamperings never seem to denote an actual mammal – as if these creatures were merely proxies for flesh and blood, a scratchy reminder. Too quick, too small, too shy to feature in creative visualisation, they meet us on the dark side of starlight, leaving our illusions intact. Laboratory pups ignore us, as does their mother with her copulatory plug in place.

1st – The Apollonian Mouse

The altar mouse enigma exercises tweedy professors. One theory is this: Apollo showed mercy in the end, inhaling the plague back into his mighty lungs, where mice continued to multiply – living memorials, two or three escaping from his mouth with every rare bombastic utterance.

2nd – The Pantry Mouse

You'd notice a lacuna in cheese but not a handful of grains missing. Omnivores look like specialists when gourmet fare is taken. The *grand cru*, mulched in Somerset with raw Friesian milk and animal rennet, wore its sackcloth for twelve hectic months. That one bite is all that was edible.

3rd – The Study Mouse

Sexing the pups is not too difficult: just lift the tails of littermates and compare perineums. When their genes are knocked out like croquet balls, a marker is introduced, making the study mouse piebald. If you see one it's a rescue escape, not a runaway dream of the bourgeois inner child.

4th – The Theatre Mouse

West End theatres are a wildlife haven. In any large, old building where people drop food, a colony may run and run. Before shows the aisles are valeted but a trap will occasionally be forgotten, left at liberty to take a life – better than snapping on a sandalled big toe, a play within a play.

5th – The Dormouse

A kindly old bat couple, unable to clamber in belfries any more, transfer their fondness to the dormouse, so appealing in the palm. Nest boxes are spaced an inch from the tree: the mice will enter only from behind. They roam the south, in search of the magic hedgerow, the northwest passage.

6th – The Hollywood Mouse

There are broad *boingggs* as a frying pan stops vibrating. The skirting board hole is impossibly far away. His eyes swivel up to the big jagged cat
    a paralysed panic. His hands are three fingered: five would have looked like a bunch of bananas (and cost the studio millions of dollars more).

All six – The Late Romantic Mouse

The empire a Russian exile loved is littered with the stone amputations of de Chirico. Milo is moonlit absence, a beauty lost in the mirror. Cars swim through the Forum, silently, to their assignations. Road mice are rare, the kestrel watchful. Which is more dangerous: black river or green verges?

63

THE TWINS

'When they complain of waking from hideous laboratory dreams, just rattle off a couple of only child anecdotes.'

Modern life has become twin-friendly — there's no longer any fear of people meeting themselves. Oddly, it's an offshoot of the cult of the individual. Few twins are defriended. Some pranksters post a single photo twice with spot-the-differences. Monozygotic double dating, covering all the bases, has gone viral. Twins' twins are happily awaited.

1st — The Twins in the Light of Day

Dee came first in the amniotic sac race, sharing a placenta with Dum. The sonographer frowned: 'Have you heard of twin-to-twin transfusion syndrome?' The Tweedles were fine in the end. They agreed to have a battle but never had one. When the monstrous crow swooped, they fled.

2nd — The Twins' Private Language

In the Idioglossia Club both life members talk pipsqueak. A linguist, like a tutor in a country house garden, strolls among blooms of sound. Ordinary siblings miss lovely chords in the den of clucks and yawns. But soon it will be catch-up time — perfect English calls to each alone in the mornings.

3rd – The Twins Making Mischief

Weight training is raw in the genes or cooked in a mythic life – either way, strident clothes are bought in stereo in identical sizes. Devilment hatches out of confidence, two to one against the suitor, borrowed as a string phone for tactless whispers, testing how Chinese they might turn out to be.

4th – The Twins in the Cavern of Dreams

Seeing double already? – a connoisseur's pint is a half-pull from each. Victorian six-way mirrors further split the zygote. In a painter's utopia in three dimensions, a maze of reflections, a sober, separate self steers us to our table by the elbow. Lookalikes in the beer cellar wink in unison.

5th – The Conjoined Twins

It's hurtful to be treated as one person – no monetary compensation could ever be enough. In any case, a meagre royalty travels twin-ward from the manager, then halves. (Discovery – while swimming one day in a Lake Geneva lido – is deemed origination in circus circles, as in scientific.)

6th – The Twins in Disguise

At carnival they glow. Rowing across the bay towards the floats, they are a species in themselves, adaptable. They are far from dimorphic: he's borrowed a patch, she a five o'clock shadow. Gender is fluid, Venetian They've gone as Marie Antoinette's tea servants, licensed to flirt.

All six – The Twins in Penury

Down on her uppers, she absents herself from personal need, giving her all to the supply side, going three or four days without food. Each twin decants a third of their meal onto a ghost plate, which holds her stare for a minute as if it were a third fatherless child materialised on her doorstep.

64

THE BOOK

'Harmony prevails when like things resonate and unlike things are in balance.'
(The Great Commentary, from the Ten Wings)

He reads to Borges in a shadowy sitting room under a Piranesi engraving:
he speaks of summer night, the conscious being of the book. A servant
is taken exploring by his blind master on a raft of text and speech. He is
asked to write the occasional note on a flyleaf – though who would read
these notes to him, and when, is not the least of the Borgesian mysteries.

1st – The Book of Splendour
The beginning gives birth to the divine – from a womb with two entrances.
Starting to create himself, the heavenly king lets brightness out of infinite
space and time. It sows a secret seed, like a silkworm enclosing itself in a
palace, named Elohim. Out of Elohim everything emerges.

2nd – The Book without Qualities
A plain brown cover may hide enough at breakfast – it will vary from
household to household. A teenager knows whether her parents might
equate blankness with chemistry, say, or Spanish. Aptly, though, she reads
about a breakfast – a slightly burnt kidney, choice offering to new gods.

3rd – The Book of Souls

The obsolete resource, torn in half by a caped showman. Why not? –
he's been hanging upside-down in a capsule for a fortnight. Pressmen
exhausted by their vigil phone in the news, some falling asleep before the
anti-climax. A demiurge with compasses, he divides the teeming city.

4th – The Book of Sameness

Antaŭparolo: Any future edition will omit the puns, the verse, and the tale
of the cannibal who ate his wife. Proverbs are nearly all from Zamenhof's
Proverbaro Esperanto. Wear the Esperanto star. Refrain from suggesting
improvements to this most beautiful language before you've learned it.

5th – The Book of Remembrance

Its inspiration is the museum – priceless, fragile exhibit, whose pages
can be turned only by a curatorial hand. A life under lock and key. You
can't flip backwards and forwards through mortalities, browsing. Nobody
minds that the daily turning is unceremonial, so long as it's never seen.

6th – The Book in Transition

Half-ghosted, the battery-powered dead float on their little skis. You touch
one, ponder lost seconds. You're on the other side, no easy route back, as
in a store with up escalators only. The new search and rejoice approach is
worse: Buffalo Bill and William Cody, darn it, are the same person!

All six – The Book of Changes

At rest, this book does not initiate. When stimulated, it's commensurate
with all causes. Actor of the force field, attune yourself to the first
stirrings, the door hinge of incipience. Find what you're looking for in the
marriage book of heaven and earth – be it faith, rectitude or pulse.

	☰	☳	☵	☶	☷	☴	☲	☱
☰	1	34	5	26	11	9	14	43
☳	25	51	3	27	24	42	21	17
☵	6	40	29	4	7	59	64	47
☶	33	62	39	52	15	53	56	31
☷	12	16	8	23	2	20	35	45
☴	44	32	48	18	46	57	50	28
☲	13	55	63	22	36	37	30	49
☱	10	54	60	41	19	61	38	58